FINDING ME IN A PAPER BAG:

Searching For Both Sides Now

WHO ARE THE PARENTS OF THIS ABANDONED BABY?

February 6, 1939

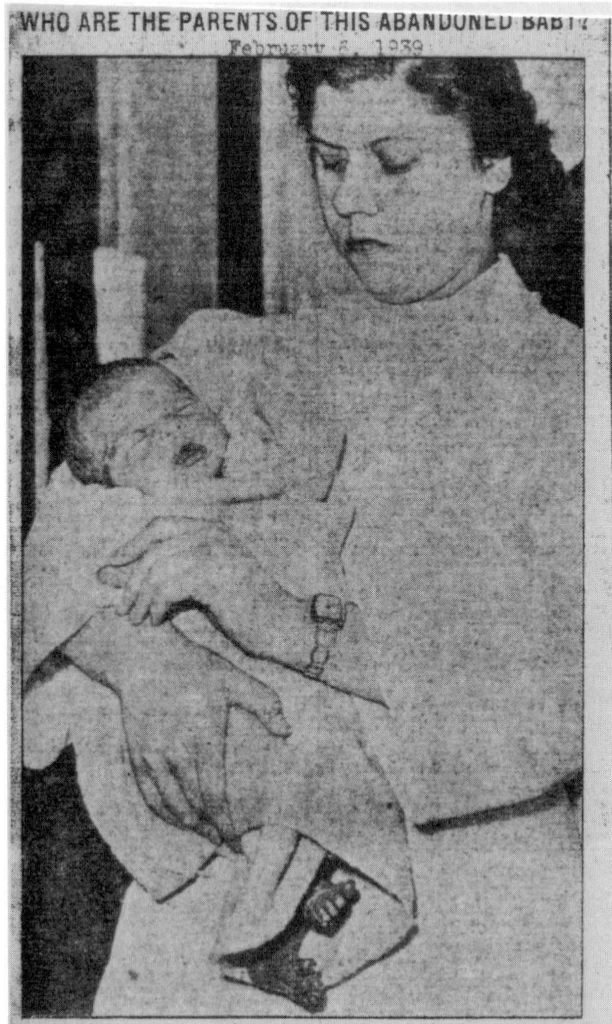

Pictured above is Miss "X," two-weeks-old baby, in the arms of one of the nurses at the York hospital where she is being cared for after havi[ng] been abandoned by her parents Sunday night on the front porch at the hon[e] of Curvin Senft, Lincoln highway, west of Thomasville. Hospital authori[ties] say the baby is in good physical condition and is gaining in weight. Co[rporal] A. B. Snyder and Private R. P. Sneeder of the criminal investi[gation] division of the Pennsylvania Motor police are conducting an investi[gation]. A description of the infant was sent out over the teletype sys[tem in an] effort to apprehend its parents.

FINDING ME IN A PAPER BAG:

Searching For Both Sides Now

Sally Howard

GATEWAY PRESS, INC.
Baltimore, MD 2003

Please direct all correspondence and book orders to:
Sally Howard
PO Box 383
San Juan Capistrano, CA 92693

Library of Congress Control Number 2003103798
ISBN 0-9740594-0-4

Published for the author by
Gateway Press, Inc.
1001 N. Calvert Street
Baltimore, MD 21202-3897

Printed in the United States of America

DEDICATION

This book is
dedicated to all those
with unknown
pasts, and to those
searching for their
truth.

ACKNOWLEDGEMENTS

Just as it takes a village to raise a child, it also takes a village to produce a book. With the help of a good editor and publisher, encouragement from family, friends, and angels, persistence and stamina, my words came to completion. With amazement I have watched the events of this adventure transpire, sometimes necessitating viewing it from afar. In those times, discouraged, depressed, confused and wanting to forget it all, someone always came into my life to guide me in my searches or to urge me on to complete my book. It is these people I wish to acknowledge.

The first person I need to thank is my husband Ross who allowed me to be depressed, obsessed, excited, then confused, and sometimes mentally empty. He kept my computer working, respected my ideas, listened to my writing and always gave encouragement. He even accompanied me to Holland to meet Liddie for the first time holding me up when I was sure I was going to fall down.

I want to thank my boys, Jay, Kiley and Daniel. While they were often confused as to why I would want to search for Liddie, a sister they never knew, or for a grandmother, who would be a stranger, they allowed me my feelings.

I want to thank my adopted brother and sister, Jon and Nancy for being there for me, supporting me in anyway needed. To my cousins, Gretchen and Eric and their families for allowing me to be free with them about my past and not judge. To my grand daughter Kalina, hopefully you will understand now why I was sad sometimes when you came to visit.

I want to thank all the birthmothers from our Internet list for their continual support. Their advice gave me clarity and sanity. They are: Billie McCabe, Reenie Brammertz, Jaye Ducan, Vicki Lawson, Audrey Dugard McVean, Mary Beth Nance, Beth Young, Mary Evans, Carolyn Flood, Janice Brewer, Pat Goodwin, Blanche Thompson, Patty Burns, Liz Lowrey, Jarrett Kroll, Holly Carhart, Pat Count-Williams, Dorene Morin, Melinda Corday, Laurie Bently Middaugh, Michelle Rice, Elaine Henwood, Peg Schultz, Judy Sullivan, Joan Poppers, Sally Fridge, Barbara Lee, Wanda Martin, Rockyisle Sue, Michelle Rice, Pam Silo and so many more. From my Full Circle group there is Cindy Shacklett, who's greatest wish was for me to publish my story, Carol Caramagno, Delayn Curtis, Bill Morrison and the rest of the regulars.

I want to thank Richard Bugler, Lieutenant Commander, United States Navy, retired, who led me in my search. Without his help I would have been lost. When I got discouraged he pushed me on or told me when I needed to back off for a while. His logic and insight were gifts.

I want to thank my friends, Beth and Marie, who, while sitting over meals, would listen as I cried, tormented over events from my past, or when I shared my happiness from new found information in my searches, always giving me encouragement telling me, "You can do it. Don't give up." Also I want to thank my friend Donna Lee, my friend from childhood who has always been supportive of anything I do. To my friends Eva and Ole, I thank you for your knowledge of foreign thinking and brilliant insights. All has been of great comfort.

To my friend Ric Canfield, I thank you for bringing humor, understanding and friendship to my dark days exactly when I needed them the most. To Jeannette I thank you for starting me on the psychic path.

To my friend Chris Oort in Holland, I thank you for your support while in Amsterdam. Welcoming me to your country and delivering me to my hotel, then knowing I could count on you if I got into trouble, was very comforting. I also thank you for your help in my search for Liddie.

To Joe Soll, you gave me the opportunity to open my soul, comforting me with knowledge that allowed me to search. Thanks for your CERA conventions.

Thanks you must go to Carol Schaefer who edited my book so professionally. At times I felt she was inside my head. Our karmic connection was unique. Also to my publisher who guided me to completion often saying to each other, "I did that, or I went there too." Another Karmic connection.

To my Red Hat Society friends, thank you for the opportunity to find out what friendship with a group of women does for your soul.

To all the other angels, psychics and others who appeared when I needed them, I thank you.

Last, but most important, is thanking my beautiful daughter Liddie a journalist and author, for allowing me in her life and for supporting me in the writing of this book. To her three children, Jet, Cato and Sal, I am glad you are in my life too. To Arjan, thank your for loving my daughter.

PREFACE

"Hi, my name is Sally. I am an adoptee, a throw away found in a paper bag. I am also a birth mother because I gave away my only daughter." Saying those words for the first time out-loud to a room full of strangers caused my life's journey to take a sharp turn. Admitting to being an adoptee was hard enough, but exposing my deeply hidden birthmother secret overwhelmed me. I honestly thought I would succumb to my newly exposed acknowledgement. Then I found, when a secret is revealed, it can no longer be stuffed back down inside. Trouble lay ahead.

Feelings I wasn't familiar with popped up leaving me confused. I was sure they were probably my adoption feelings rearing their ugly heads so I found an adoption therapist. In the meantime, in order to survive mentally, I started pounding away at my computer. As I purged my adoption feelings on paper I figured, if I got to an emotion I didn't understand, I could have it taken care of at the therapist's office. It was almost like I was giving myself permission to write.

One day, at a session, knowing she had read my first one hundred pages, I felt our time that day would be spent working on issues exposed in my writing. Instead, all she said, as she dropped the manila folder carrying my words on her desk was, "You have the makings of a story here." Well, the seed was planted.

Searching, I found out, started my long postponed grieving process - a process I had kept on hold for so many years. How could I grieve for my mother or daughter? To do so would have meant they were dead. Throughout the book I experienced all seven stages of recovery: "Denial, survival, awakening, grief work, bargaining, forgiveness and transformation."

Running across Joni's Mitchell's song, Both Sides Now, her words, "I really don't know life at all," depicted how I felt before I started to search. The words also spoke volumes about my feelings during my search too, as I was constantly bantered emotionally from either the adoptee side or the birthparent side. What I thought was truth, in the adoption and birth parent mode, constantly changed, making me feel like I really didn't know life at all.

I thought being a birth mother would help me understand my daughter's feelings, but found they only got in the way. When I got in the birth mother mode, my deeply seated adoption feelings over rode them. As I continued to search, the pounding inside my head was constant. Trying to find peace through understand at the end of the tunnel of confusion became my goal. Bookstores and support group meeting became my home away from home.

My story includes angels, and psychics giving me help and direction, an international search using the new confidential intermediary system through the courts in Michigan, and involvement with the Catholic Church.

Knowing each person sees events in life through their own eyes, my story is just that, 'my' story. It is what it was like for me, being an adoptee: one having no birthday, no nationality, and no paper trail to start a search, living my life as a foundling. It will show what 'Safe Haven" babies will face being alive but unknown. It will also show the emotional aftermath of giving away an only daughter to strangers, a tightly held secret for over thirty-five years.

While my story is about adoption and relinquishment, it is also for anyone carrying the heavy load of a secret. I hope the research I did and the recording of my honest feelings will help other to not be afraid to face their fears, to know that on the other side of those paralyzing apprehensions is completeness, truth and most times, joy.

Sixty some years later I have been able to poke my way out of that paper bag I was abandoned in and find 'ME.' The journey was hard, but as an adoptee and birth parent, I thank God every day that I can now, more clearly then ever, understand what life is all about, from 'Both Sides Now.'

PROLOGUE

It had been a long day and Farmer Sundy was tired. Glad to be done with his chores before nightfall, he secured the barn door and headed home. As he started across the highway, he noticed a strange sedan pulling up in front of his house. Sundy knew who owned all of the automobiles in the vicinity, and this one was not familiar.

In the distance, Sundy watched transfixed as a woman emerged from the passenger side of the car, carrying a large paper bag. Rushing up to the porch, the woman furtively glanced around, then carefully placed the bag by the lighted window. Turning back, she spotted Sundy approaching her. Quickly retrieving the bag, she raced back to the car and climbed in. Before the door was firmly shut, the male driver pulled the car back onto the highway, squealing tires kicking up dust.

Sundy grabbed a twig lying at his feet and scrawled as much of the license plate numbers as he could remember into the cold, wet ground. The plates were from Maryland, just across the state border near his Pennsylvania farm.

Speeding down the remote two-lane highway, the car barely slowed as it bounced over the railroad tracks, then quickly pulled over and stopped at the next farmhouse with lights on. Holding the bag close, the woman dashed up to the porch, finally able to finish what she started. Hurrying back to the car, she pulled her thin coat closer and allowed herself one last glance back at the bag, now half bathed in light by the lamp in the window.

In the parlor toward the back of the house, thirteen-year-old Janet Senft and her younger sister were playing the piano and singing.

Hearing a strange crying sound from outside, Janet paused. "It sounds like a cat is in distress. Maybe it's somehow stuck in the fence. Listen, don't you hear it?"

"I don't hear anything," her sister answered. "Let's keep singing."

But Janet felt compelled to follow the sound. The strange cries drew her outside to the porch where she discovered a large, brown paper bag. Figuring someone dropped off a kitten, she was shocked to see a tiny baby inside the bag instead. Janet hollered for her dad.

Mr. Senft rushed the baby into the warmth of the house and called to his sick wife to come downstairs right away.

"Can we keep it?" Janet immediately began pleading. All she wanted in the world was to keep the baby.

"We already have enough children," her father explained. "We need to call the police. This baby needs its mother."

While Mr. Senft left the room to phone the Pennsylvania State Police, Mrs. Senft checked the baby to make sure it was all right. Her other children gathered around closer to get a better look. Unwrapping the blanket, she said softly, "It's a little girl. She seems healthy."

The children began asking questions all at once. "Why would someone leave their baby out in the cold in the middle of winter?" "Can I hold her?" "Why can't we keep her?" "Can we please keep her?"

Interrupting the commotion, Mr. Senft announced, "The police said I must take the baby to York Hospital." After asking his neighbor to ride with him, Mr. Senft wrapped the baby back up in her blankets, grabbed the paper bag holding possible evidence and left for the hospital.

On arrival, the tiny infant was placed in semi-isolation so as not to risk possibly infecting the other newborns with a communicable disease. Having no idea where the baby came from, they couldn't put the hospital and patients in jeopardy.

During her six-week stay, while social services tried to find her parents, the nurses became very attached to the abandoned baby girl. At first, it was challenging to find a formula that she could keep down, but finally one was found. One student nurse, unable to fathom a child having no name, called her Judy. All the student nurses took turns loving and mothering tiny Judy.

* * * * * * * *

In the town of Carlisle, about an hour drive from the hospital, Doctor and Mrs. Miller each took a section of the evening paper to read. As was their habit, he took the sports section, she the front page. Not expecting much in the way of exciting news in their sleepy little town, Mrs. Miller reacted with shock to the story about the little baby girl found on a farmhouse porch.

"Listen to this," she said to her husband, and proceeded to read him the entire article. "How could anyone do such a thing? Here we are, still mourning the death of our precious Mary Caroline - the child we waited eight years to have! This baby has nothing wrong with her, and she's abandoned in a brown paper bag. What if she had had Spinal Bifida like our little girl? What would the parents have done then? Life's just not fair."

Still deep in their grief, the Millers were powerfully drawn to this little baby, who needed a home as much as they felt they needed a baby to fill their horrible loss. Through their lawyer, they arranged a visit.

Walking into the nursery's isolation unit, Dr. Miller took one look at little Judy, now sick with bronchitis, and pronounced, "This child needs to be fattened up. Why the skin just hangs from her bones."

There was no doubt in their minds that this would be their child. But first, Mrs. Miller wanted to visit the home where the baby was found.

Sitting together in the farmhouse living room, Mrs. Miller asked Mrs. Senft what she thought of the baby when they found her.

Puzzled at the question, Mrs. Senft responded, "All I know is she seemed healthy the little I saw of her."

Satisfied, Mrs. Miller spoke quietly, "Please don't tell anyone, but we're going to adopt her. We want the chance to tell her ourselves, at the right time, how she came to us."

The promise made, the adoption went on to completion. In March of 1939, Judy had new parents, a new home, and a new name: Sarah Jeanette Miller.

I was always called Sally.

CHAPTER ONE

"What we need to talk to you about is your beginnings," is how my mother began the discussion when I was five. The sight of my parents sitting so close to each other on the couch, looking very serious, alarmed me. They never sat that close on the couch. But, there was my dad, all six foot four inches of him, snuggled right up next to my petite five foot four inch mother. Maybe if there hadn't been such an extreme contrast between their sizes, I might not have been so struck by the sight. But somehow I sensed before a word was said that my whole world was about to change forever.

We had just moved to a bigger house. Our first home was a three-story building located near the town square, the business center of historical Carlisle, Pennsylvania. My father's dental practice took up the front part of the main floor of the building. On the third floor was my mother's nursery school, and the rest of the building served as our living quarters.

While we lived there, my mother gave birth to my sister Nancy and my brother Jonathan. I remember being so happy to have company and looking forward to the time they would join my daily excursions up and down the wooden stairs, shiny from layers of lacquer and made safe with treads of rubber. Those stairs led to all the important places in my young life. Going downstairs I was in the security of my dad's office. Upstairs led to Mom. Sometimes, while climbing those stairs, each one was counted very slowly, as I anticipated the punishment awaiting me for roaming too far from home.

Whenever I returned home after one of my little forbidden excursions, the first thing I saw as I opened the front door was the patients filling the red chrome-trimmed furniture in my dad's waiting room. The Saturday Evening Posts, with their Norman Rockwell covers, and the most recent Life Magazines on the coffee table were always in disarray. When office hours were over, it was my job to straighten the magazines, which I did with great zeal.

I played for hours in the backyard, only a few feet away from where my dad was seeing patients. While I made mud pies in the cups of my little tin tea set, the breeze dried the mixed array of clothes strung on the clothesline. The long line was propped up by two-by-fours, cut at the top with notches by my dad, to prevent the line from sagging. Finished "cooking," I would set my pies out to dry on the top of the cellar door.

In 1943, after the United States entered the war, discussions became endless about whether we had enough coupons. There were rations on sugar, coffee, meats, cheese, flour and many other things. Each family received a book of coupons amounting to points, which gave them the right to buy certain items.

But it was the different-colored ration tokens that my mother kept in the change pocket of her wallet that I found more interesting, since they bought oleo margarine. My sister and I always argued over whom was going to get to burst the orange dot inside the plastic bag filled with a white Crisco-looking substance. Once the orange was released and kneaded into the rest, the oleo became the color of butter. Each time was magic.

The constant air raid sounds scared me. As soon as the siren's low moan began, everyone stopped what they were doing, turned off the lights and closed the blinds. By the time the sound escalated to a high pitch, we were all immersed in total darkness. The silence of that darkness caused us all to talk in whispers.

When, in my small voice, I asked my mother why everything had to be dark, she explained, "In case enemy airplanes are flying over us. We hope, if they don't see any lights on, they will keep on flying by and not bomb us."

My imagination ran wild when I was sitting in the dark. Even if the sirens weren't blaring, I feared a plane might bomb us if someone left the light on in the bathroom. Sometimes I hid under my bed, feeling the comforting darkness offered more safety.

Our college town had many monuments to war. The area had been vital to Americans fighting during the Revolutionary and Civil Wars. Nicks on the old courthouse from cannon balls were part of the lore. The Carlisle Army War College was the oldest army post in the United States. A life-size statue of Mollie Pitcher, the woman who helped the soldiers in the Battle of Monmouth in 1778, stands in the local cemetery among tombstones dating from the 1700's. History permeated the town, and, along with the ambiance from being a college town, it lent a sense of safety and a solid foundation for bringing up children. I loved living there.

The new home I moved to when I was five was in a more residential neighborhood and was registered with the Historical Society as one of the homes "built for the elite" in 1910. Four stories tall if you counted the basement, the house had a big yard with a wraparound front porch overlooking its corner lot. The rooms were all large. Nancy and I shared a bedroom. I was excited about my new home and exploring a new neighborhood.

That day that my life was to forever change, I was busy playing in the dining room when my mother called out for me to come into the living room. I was certain I had done something wrong again.

With Dad close by her side on the couch, Mom began to tell me about how I had come into their family in a special way - not the way my brother and sister had come. "We got to pick you out," she said. "You were chosen. With your brother and sister, we had to take what we got. With you, because we chose you, it makes you very special."

What they were saying? Pick me out? Why would they pick me out? Was I for sale or something?

All of a sudden, everything went funny in my head. My heart seemed to slow down, and I stopped listening. My parents continued talking. I could see their mouths were still moving, but I was in some other place. All that I remembered was something about a bag, and that I was found in it. My real mother left me in a brown paper bag? But how could she have? Wasn't what they were saying just a big mistake? This makes me different from my sister and baby brother! If I am different from them, then who are these people who are talking to me? Maybe they will give me away, too, if I'm not good? I'm feeling so sad, and I don't want to hear any more about this, or ever, ever think about it ever again.

And I didn't. As if trying to be born anew, I split off from that part of myself they just told me about and left it all behind like it was only a bad dream that I had to forget. I wasn't left by my real mother in a brown paper bag. No way! This was maybe something that had happened to Sarah Jeanette. But, how could such a story be possibly true for Sally?

*   *   *   *   *   *   *   *

One day soon after, my mother announced cheerily, "Guess what! Today, you are going to get to visit Uncle Russell's office at Dickinson College and play games! He's coming to pick you up!" I was told my Uncle Russell was a psychologist, but I was too young at the time to know what that meant. Even so, somehow it sounded important. Eager for my big outing, I was ready long before he arrived.

It was fun at his office. While I placed the wooden shapes into the correct holes, he would watch and then push in the stem of his pocket watch. My favorite game was telling him what the pictures he held up meant. From his constant smile, I knew I was pleasing him.

As we were leaving the brownstone building to go home, Uncle Russell leaned down to me and said, "I don't know why your mother wanted you tested. Why there is nothing wrong with you. You are a darling, normal, healthy child."

Normal? Healthy? I had no idea what he was talking about. Tested? I thought we were playing games. Did my mother think there was something wrong with me? Suddenly, I felt the same hurt in my heart as when I learned about being left in a paper bag. But, I quickly pushed those feelings far away for Sarah to have.

*　*　*　*　*　*　*　*

My mother's attempts to soothe me about the story of how I came to be in their family had the opposite effect. "Sally," she said one day. " Have you ever heard the story about the Little Match Girl by Hans Christian Anderson? It's such a sad story. You know, you are our little match girl."

Pulling the book down from the shelf, she patted the spot on the couch next to her where she wanted me to sit. As I listened intently to the story, I wondered how this little girl was like me? She was so poor she had to sell matches to earn money. She was all alone, and it was dark outside. Where were her parents? Look at her clothes. They are all ripped and dirty. She didn't seem like me at all!

Looking at the picture of the Little Match Girl standing in the cold all alone made me so angry. Needing to understand, I exclaimed, "She can see the rich family having their New Year's feast, so why doesn't she just go and bang on their window!" But, then I realized the Little Match Girl had frozen to death totally alone in the snow.

Closing the book, my mother pulled me close and said, "See, you were outside in the cold, too, just like the Little Match Girl. But, we took you in."

* * * * * * * *

For the next five years, until I was ten, I managed to forget all about my beginnings. My mother's early attempts at consoling me subsided. But then one day, by accident, I was forced again to remember.

My chore that day was to clean the upstairs. Much preferring to clean the downstairs because it was easier, I was racing through the job of dusting my parents' bedroom furniture. In my rush, I pulled out the tiny middle drawer of their desk to shove something away in it. Tucked into the drawer was a newspaper clipping that caught my attention. As I glanced over it, I realized it was about me.

Carrying the article in the palm of my hand as if I were carrying the holy grail, I sat down on the edge of the bed to read it. The clipping was dated February 8, 1939.

Baby Abandoned on Hanover Porch

> A girl baby between one and two weeks old was abandoned Monday evening at 7:50 o'clock on the front porch of Curwin Senft's residence, Lincoln Highway, just west of Thomasville. Mr. Senft found the baby in a brown paper shopping bag. The baby was taken to York hospital where it was reported in good condition.

In shock, I read the article over and over and over. It was true. It wasn't a made up story. The word abandoned created an explosion in my brain that traveled through my body. The beating of my heart was so strong and pumped my blood with so much force that I literally could not hear a thing except my own now incessant thoughts: "You are adopted. Your mother threw you away. Threw you away!"

I felt like a very different person as I slowly walked back over to the desk to tuck the clipping back into its little hiding place in the middle drawer. Knowing suicide would be impossible for me to carry out, I walked around from then on with a chip on my shoulder and developed an attitude to carry me through. My plan was to become someone famous, so that no one would ever have such power over my life ever again.

* * * * * * * *

Upon entering adolescence, I developed eczema. The severe itching caused the skin on the inside bend of my elbows to ooze. I was dragged from one specialist to another as we sought answers, not just for the eczema but also for my continual bed-wetting. At age fifteen, I developed a spastic colon.

Eat raisins in the evening and have no water after six, was suggested by one specialist for the bed-wetting. Various salves were prescribed for my eczema, and I was not to drink cokes to cure my spastic colon. Then ulcers developed in my mouth, which would come and go. No real cures for any of my troubles were found. Instead, I chose to avoid certain situations, like sleepovers for fear of wetting the bed. Besides, all the excitement would cause my stomach to seize up anyway.

Being a year younger than most in my class, getting good grades was really hard work. Keeping up with the latest fashions and running with the popular crowd was much easier. As a member of the band, I played the clarinet or the drums during the concert season, marching in the band front as a flag twirler during football season. I sang in the church and school choirs, took piano lessons and was elected president of Luther League at church. All were normal activities for someone my age, but I never felt normal and free to be myself except when I was attending our Lutheran church camp.

At Camp Nawakwa, no one knew I was adopted. Feeling free to blend in, I excelled, winning swimming meets, performing in skits, and was chosen to be tribal chief over a large number of girls. Most mornings, I awoke early and sat peacefully alone under a pine tree free to meditate or read my Bible.

Then one afternoon, my terribly homesick cousin, Sue, stood sobbing before one of the counselors. In the midst of planning a stone ceremony with the other tribal chiefs, I looked up and noticed my cousin's distress.

Hoping to comfort Sue, the counselor brought her over to the group and said, "Sally, why don't you tell your cousin why you like camp so much."

To my horror, Sue screamed out, "What does she know? She's nothing but an adopted brat!"

If I stayed there a moment longer, I knew I would be devoured by what I came to call the "evil adoption shadow man." So I ran and ran, and I didn't care where I was going. I just had to get away from that word adopted. Finding myself in unfamiliar mountain terrain, I didn't care. Being lost and dying seemed like a far better alternative to having to face all my friends, who now knew my awful secret. I was illegitimate. My mother threw me away!

Tripping over tree roots and loose pine cones, I just kept going. But, then out of the corner of my eye, I spotted one of the counselors, nearly out of breath, trying to catch up to me. "Please, give me a minute," she was yelling.

Still running, I yelled over my shoulder, "I'm never going back to that camp, not ever! I don't care what you say. You can't make me. Go away!"

In the midst of my turmoil, I felt the quietness of the woods. The counselor's shouted words reached me through that quiet. "I am adopted, too. I know how you feel."

Stunned, I stopped running. Someone else has this problem? What sort of creature was this? I wasn't alone?

Darkness had fallen by the time we finished talking over our feelings about being adopted and returned to camp. Counselors and the head of the camp ran out of the staff's A-frame building to greet us. My parents were called and assured that all was under control, and I was fine.

But, I wasn't fine. I no longer had a sanctuary from being adopted.

* * * * * * * *

"For heavens sake, Tiny! Don't you know your own daughter's name?" Dad had picked up my learner's permit from the Department of Motor Vehicles and had spelled my name wrong. He shrugged his big shoulders in confusion. "You forgot to add the "h" to Sarah!"

With a strange detachment, I looked at the misspelling and thought to myself, "Sarah or Sara. What does it matter? I never go by Sarah anyway. Judy is dead. Sarah is dead. This just proves it." Later, seeing the misspelling on the permanent license was like witnessing a false brand on a stolen cow. I had not known how to correct the spelling, so my driver's license became another icon of my identity crises.

Often, while sitting before the triple mirror of my antique vanity, I found myself wondering whom it was I did look like. Turning back and forth from one mirror to the other, I only saw the only familiar image I knew- my own. Realizing I probably would never know another who would mirror me, I often pushed my bench away and got up from my musings in disgust.

Where it was all right for me to wonder about my heritage, it felt like sport when others did. All I wanted was to belong, to be a part of my adoptive family, not some mysterious member. I just wanted to be normal. Aunt Rachel, my mother's twin, speculated that my phantom mother was a dancer because my legs were so muscular. My mom added she was probably musically inclined as well. Even if they were being liberal talking about a taboo subject, I wanted to scream. All their talk did was intensify my differences.

My mother's behavior toward me was growing abusive. Once, she used a willow switch from the tree in the front yard, leaves stripped, to punish Nancy and me for goofing off and not packing our bags for our annual summer vacation at the Jersey shore. The stinging whips quickly caused Nancy to shrink to the other side of the room. As usual, I confronted my mother's abuse, but my mother's rampage continued until she was spent and I retreated with Nancy to the corner of the room. The welts on my body swelled and the deep scratches reddened. I could not imagine how I was going to wear a bathing suit. With hate in my heart, I packed my suitcase and crawled into bed, hoping a miracle would make my wounds disappear.

My mother would read my mail and listened to my phone calls as if, I believed, she was looking for something evil in me. Once she warned me not to see the movie The Bad Seed, as it would not be good for me. The film would have never played locally anyway. From puberty on, my mother was afraid of my sexuality. Despite the fact that she knew and really liked my first boyfriend, Lenny, my first great love, she never trusted me and never saw my innocence.

Once I found myself flung across the kitchen, when I dared to wipe under her plate while she was still eating, so I could be finished with the last of my chores and meet my friends to buy the weekly 45 record picks. Pain seared my head. Astonished that she could hurt me so brutally, I realized she had backhanded me across my face with her huge diamond ring. I was blinded with a rage I had never felt before. The next thing I knew, I was straddling my mother on the floor wanting to kill her. Somehow, in that moment, I remembered there was a fine line between love and hate and, if the line was ever crossed, jail could be the result.

I stopped. Instead, I screamed, "You will never, ever hurt me again. I'm sick of you always putting me down. I'm sick of never being good enough, of always being your whipping boy. Let's see if you tell Daddy what you did this time. I am sick of you calling me a whore, reading my mail, and listening in on my phone conversations. All these things will never happen again, or I will hurt you like you hurt me! I will leave home, run away."

To validate the pain I was feeling, I tore over to the mirror and looked at my reflection. All the blood vessels in my eye were broken. Like a wounded animal, I retreated to my bedroom, emotionally beaten. Why could I not fit into this family?

* * * * * * * *

Finally, I was able to run away with permission. It was expected of me to attend college, as everyone in the Miller family had. I applied as a music major to West Chester State College, near Philadelphia. When, after passing my piano, voice and instrument auditions, I stumbled on the theory exam, it was decided I should major in elementary education. Just like my mother.

For months, we had been filling the trunk with necessities. Breathing a sigh of relief that the trunk lid of our car could actually close over it, I wrapped a scarf over my hair, knotted it in the back, slid on my Foster Grant polarized sunglasses and climbed into the car. I was so ready, and so happy to be leaving home.

However, my adoption issues came along with me to school, and college did not turn out to be the happy place I had thought it would be. The feeling of being out of place and of not belonging, of everyone seeming to be smarter and more talented than me, followed me there. Despite working hard to get good grades in order to make my mother proud, I found myself freezing up in exams even though I knew the material. Soon I was on probation, and I began to sleep all the time.

Then one day, while reading Glamour Magazine, I came across an ad for an airline school and something just clicked. The idea of learning about the world first hand and getting paid for it was very appealing. As I sent away for the application for stewardess training at McConnell Airline School, I just knew I would be accepted.

Months of begging and pleading with my mother to be allowed to come home from college had fallen on deaf ears. Now I called dad and convinced him. When he came to pick me up, I told him my life was heading in a new direction. Feeling that this was something I would really succeed in made me feel good about myself.

On the flight to begin training, I visualized myself in a smart-looking uniform, succeeding on my own. It wasn't until I arrived that I learned I was too young to fly and had to enter the ground agent class. But I didn't want ground training. I wanted to fly! When they felt they had made it clear that the stewardess training would not lead to a job right away, they allowed me to take the training anyway.

Toward the end of training, my teacher suggested I go on an interview just for the experience. Feeling no pressure knowing I couldn't be hired, I was comfortable as the interviewer ran through his list of questions. But his final "test" was unnerving. He asked me to walk for him, motioning me to twirl several times. Then he asked me to lift my skirt, then lift it higher. Were all the girls asked to do the same? I was suddenly relieved to have the interview over.

Back at home waiting to become of age, I filled out applications every evening after work, hoping to find an airline that hired at eighteen. My dream came true when Mohawk Airlines accepted me into their training class when I turned eighteen and a half.

After an intense month of training, I was just about to graduate when, at lunch with my classmates, I was told that in order to graduate the teacher had to be allowed to snap my bra and girdle. Livid at hearing this, I was determined I was not going to be humiliated, like I had been on my first interview when I had to hike my skirt up so high. I had worked too hard to be demeaned by this type of behavior.

Back in class that afternoon, I couldn't get the rumor out of my mind, so I raised my hand to ask the teacher if it were true.

With a smirk he responded, "Yeah. So what? Can't you take it?"

He made my skin crawl. "You're not going to touch me!" I told him and, not believing what I was doing, I picked up my things and walked out the door. Where did I think I was going?

Back home, each night in my bedroom I again went through the process of applying for a stewardess job, still handicapped by my age. Twenty-one was the age limit for most airlines. Then North Central Airlines called me, having received my name from McConnell. Flying home from their exam in Minneapolis, I found myself on pins and needles. Would I be accepted into their program? If so, I knew I would have to wait two weeks after graduation, when I became nineteen and a half, to begin to fly. The call finally came. Out of a field of three hundred applicants, thirteen of us were accepted for the next class.

Never had I worked so hard, and, when they pinned my wings onto my uniform, I thought I would burst with pride. The class scattered to their various home bases. I had chosen Detroit because it was closest to home. As I waited for my two weeks to be up to fly, I watched my roommates return from their first flights, a slight green pallor to their skin. Both had become terribly air sick. Would that happen to me?

My day finally arrived. As I checked my appearance in the bathroom mirror, I felt the brown gabardine uniform issued for summer, with its crisp white shirt underneath, looked just perfect. As I secured the matching hat with bobbi pins, my eye caught the sparkle of my wings as the light hit it just right. Even having to wear the mandatory girdle and nylons could not dispel my joy. Finally slipping into my brown and white spectator high heels, I announced to no one in particular as I left my room, "Now, I am ready to go!"

Upon arriving at the airport, I blithely proceeded to the wrong plane. I had to laugh at myself for assuming I was already quite sophisticated! At least I didn't get air sick later.

CHAPTER TWO

Flying was all I hoped it would be, and I relished my new role. There was no way I would have guessed that in a short while my whole life would take a devastating turn.

Needing a change of scenery, I applied for a transfer to the base in Madison, Wisconsin. After getting settled, the airlines requested that I attend a dinner being held for investors. I was to mingle with the guests and be sociable. It was there that I met John, a senior law student, who was sitting at the bar. For the next few months we dated. Troubles were apparent right away. Though lots of fun, John was a heavy drinker. In those months, as I attempted to fit in with the senior crew based in Madison, I began to realize that their standoffishness toward a junior new member of the crew was not going to go away. And neither was John's drinking. So I requested a transfer back to Detroit.

But back in Detroit, I found myself missing John. When he told me he was only interested in furthering his career and had no time for a relationship, I was temporarily crushed. But I knew he was probably too deep into the bottle to really care about anything. Lenny, my boyfriend from high school was really my great love, but when I couldn't make a commitment, he joined the service. Something in me always resisted being attached to anyone. Since Lenny and I began dating when I was fifteen, our relationship had been on again off again. Finally, after I joined the airlines, he had had enough.

The next months were lonely. I had no desire to date, and my roommate went home for a month to have an operation. It was after a routine round trip flight from Detroit to

Chicago, while my roommate was still away, that I met the man who would forever change the course of my life, in the most destructive way.

Heading for the stewardess lounge to check my mailbox and flying schedule before going home, I suddenly realized I had left my purse in our airline lounge in Chicago. Operations was notified and, with no money and no house keys, I had two hours to kill until the next flight from Chicago arrived with my purse.

Knowing Al Green's restaurant would extend me credit, I headed there for a cup of coffee. While sipping my coffee, I couldn't help noticing the tall man in a trench coat standing at the bar staring at me. Finally, he walked over to my table and introduced himself. "Hi, my name is Hugh," he said. "May I join you." With two hours stretching before me, I thought, "Why not?"

During the course of our conversation, he said that he was in Detroit delivering a fleet of cars. Not surprising for Detroit. Did I go into the city very often he wondered? I told him my girlfriends and I often took the airport limousine in for shopping and dinner. So, he asked to take me to dinner sometime, and I gave him my phone number. He seemed harmless, and I was glad of the prospect of company with my roommate gone.

Not long afterwards he called, and a place to meet for dinner was arranged. It was an easy walk to the restaurant from the airport limousine's first stop at the Sheraton Hotel. I was right on time. But, after an hour waiting for Hugh, the bartender said I had to face it, I'd been stood up. Never having been stood up before, I believed something serious had happened. The limo back to the airport had already left, so I had no other option but to wait for the next one. My return ticket was already purchased.

Finally, Hugh arrived, out of breath and full of apologies. He hadn't been able to leave a meeting and now could only spend a couple of hours because he had to cover later for a salesman, whose father had a heart attack. Someone was arriving from Indiana for a car he'd ordered. "I'm so sorry," he said. "I'll make it up to you, I promise."

Waiving the waiter over, he said, "Give the lady what she wants to eat. For me, I only want a drink. I've already eaten."

This was supposed to be a dinner date, and I felt really uncomfortable eating alone. But, Hugh didn't seem to mind at all. He chatted away, enjoying another drink, acting as if all was right with the world.

Within minutes of finishing my meal, he offered to drive me home. "It's the least I can do, since I kept you waiting for so long," he explained. Despite my protests, he insisted, placing a wad of money on the table to cover the bill.

During the forty-five minute trip to my place, we discovered we had something in common - we were both adopted. While we were engrossed in discussing adoption, I noticed Hugh was yawning a lot. He didn't seem drunk. Arriving at my place, we had the obligatory good night kiss in the car. As I turned to leave, Hugh yawned and stretched again as if exhausted. I couldn't let him drive back to the city that tired so I invited him in for a cup of strong black coffee for the road.

As we entered my rented mobile home, I dropped my purse on the kitchen table and headed toward the stove. "Coffee will be ready in a minute," I called out, going through the ritualistic steps of filling the aluminum percolator pot with tap water, measuring in the right amount of coffee into the basket and twisting the lid tight. As I bent to check the gas flame, Hugh suddenly swept me up from behind and carried me off to my roommate's bedroom.

My mind raced over all my options. Would anyone hear me if I screamed? I didn't recall seeing lights on next door. I wanted to fight him off, but he was way too big. Hugh threw me onto the bed, forcing me into a spread eagle position. The weight of his two hundred and thirty pound body overwhelmed me. I could barely breath, and I couldn't move a muscle. I prayed for a way to get my hands free.

Then suddenly one hand was freed when he released it to pull up my dress and tug down my underwear. Using strength I had no idea I was capable of, I pushed as hard as I could on his chest. For a moment he stopped. He was angry and proceeded to show me who was boss. My free arm was slammed back over my head. Nothing was going to stop him.

Feeling like a cornered animal, all my instincts were on high alert. Adrenalin coursed through my body. Frozen, I waited for any slight movement from him that would allow me to get free.

Again, he needed to release my arm, and I began thrashing about, but to no avail. The dead weight of his six foot two body kept me from moving at all. Finally, I stopped struggling and turned my face to the wall as he forced himself into me. I found myself floating above our bodies. There was no sound as I observed the scene. Was I dead? The man satisfied himself. The girl's body was still. But then she was me again. I was still alive.

Having no idea what to do, I went to the kitchen to pour him the promised coffee. He leaned his large frame against the bedroom door and asked with a smirk, "Why did you fight so hard?"

I couldn't find my voice to respond. I couldn't find my spirit to do anything about what just happened. The experience left a bitter taste in my mouth. As I stood at the stove, my back to him, all I could do was swallow my feeling from it all.

* * * * * * * *

My period was late. After a flight, during which I had terrible cramps, my friend Captain Harvey rushed me to the emergency room. I was told I had a kidney infection and given pills which did not help. Two days later, the cramps were back. Having no doctor of my own, Captain Harvey ordered me to call his, who referred to someone else, a Dr. Sullivan. After a thorough exam, Dr. Sullivan said I could very well be pregnant, but it was too soon to know for sure. I went home to wait to see if the rabbit died. No rabbit ever had so many prayers to keep it alive.

What was I to do if the worst case were true? What would my parents think? For certain they'd believe they had not raise me properly. Would I lose my job? This was not the way my life was supposed to go. A woman needs to be married to have a baby.

Dr. Sullivan's office called, asking me to make an appointment, an ominous sign, but I kept praying anyway. Before taking a seat in the waiting room, I turned my class ring around to look like a wedding band. Still praying for that rabbit, I was sitting on the edge of the examining room table when the doctor burst in. "Congratulations, Mrs. Miller. You're pregnant!"

I burst into tears.

Dr. Sullivan rushed to assure me, "Your husband will be thrilled to be a dad."

"No," I told him. "I'm not married. I don't even know the man. I feel like an outcast."

Dr. Sullivan stressed I didn't have to feel like an outcast. "This happens to the best of girls. Mistakes happen. You will have to suffer, but after it is all over, you can lead a normal life like everyone else."

Nothing he said made sense. All I worried about was what people would think, especially my parents.

He advised me not to marry "the fellow" just for the sake of the baby. It was then that I told him I had been taken advantage of. Angry now himself, he proposed a plan.

"Girls that aren't married just don't have babies," he said. This I knew to be true. Often they disappeared, never to be seen again.

His plan was to get me a valid excuse not to fly because of ear problems. I walked out of the office with a written explanation to his friend, the ear specialist, about my situation. The envelope was sealed. It was a relief having someone who knew what to do.

Hiding my secret was hard work. Airline policy in those days demanded that stewardesses be grounded without pay for being even a few pounds overweight. I wanted to fly for as long as my uniform could fit, so naturally I was hypersensitive to any comments about my weight. When one passenger offered me a candy bar and then, in fun, took back the offer saying I looked like I had put on a few pounds, I nearly burst into tears.

Finally, I needed to confide in somebody and I told Captain Harvey. Without hesitating, he gave me the number for his attorney. "What Hugh did to you is wrong," he stated. "And he should have to pay." Though I did want revenge, I did nothing.

After missing my next period, I could no longer stay in denial. Dr. Sullivan phoned and asked me to come in to see him. Pulling his chair closer to me he said, "I know a wonderful woman, a social worker in Ann Arbor, who has dealt with many cases like yours." He gave me her name and number and asked me to make an appointment with him in a month for a checkup.

* * * * * * * *

Returning to home base after a long hot flight, I was straightening up the cabin when an agent who had come on board commented that I was sure getting fat. I sassed him back, but I knew the time had finally come for me to stop flying. Now that I was almost five months pregnant, the button on my waste band could no longer close. It was time to set the inevitable in motion.

First, I made the appointment with the ear specialist. When I handed him the letter from Dr. Sullivan, he said he had been expecting me. Apparently they had already been talking about my situation. After quickly reading through the letter, he signed it and wished me good luck. He was very kind. But, I'm afraid I needed much more than good luck.

The airlines gave me an immediate leave of absence. Captain Harvey suggested I move in with his family, but my roommate and I decided to move to Detroit and not let anyone know. We found a nice basement apartment with its own private entrance off the street. The one drawback was the overhead pipes that hung too low for tall visitors.

In a nearby convenience store, to purchase some necessities, my roommate and I were approached by two policemen. I was afraid trouble was brewing, but they were inquiring about whether or not we were lost. "You are in a rough neighborhood," one of them told us. "You shouldn't be here. Buy your things, and we'll escort you home."

The officers became friends, my angels in disguise, my only contact with the outside world. Often, I would hear the doorbell ring and, when I went to the door, no one would be there. But a bag of burgers from White Castle would be left on the mat.

Once, the bell didn't ring but there was a knock at the door. Afraid someone from the airlines had tracked me down, I peaked through the window and saw instead, a stranger.

The woman introduced herself as Mrs. Wessinger, a social worker from Children's Aid Society. She asked if she could come in?"

Thrilled to have company, I saw no harm. As it turned out, she was the friend Dr. Sullivan's had mentioned. He had contacted her, feeling I might need someone to talk with about my situation. There seemed no harm in listening to what she had to say.

Since I was single and pregnant, my health insurance would not cover my medical needs, Mrs. Wessinger informed me. She urged me to go to Hugh for my expenses: rent, food and medical coverage. I was shocked. To that point my only concern had been in hiding my condition. I had not gotten even so far as to think about medical coverage. She seemed to know what to do, so I agreed to have her help me.

*   *   *   *   *   *   *   *

After a couple of weeks, I heard from Mrs. Wessinger again. She had contacted Hugh and wanted me to go with her the next day to meet with him and discuss my financial needs. How did she ever find out where he worked?

We pulled up to a dealership. I waited in the car as Mrs. Wessinger went in search of Hugh. Her first inquiry was met with a sarcastic response that Hugh was out of town. Not believing him for a moment, Mrs. Wessinger marched into the office and learned he would be returning in a few minutes from delivering a car to New York City. "Let him know we will be at the restaurant down the street. He will know what the meeting is about," she commanded.

On pins and needles and smoking way too much, I was scared to death to see Hugh again and amazed when he actually showed up. He suggested a quieter restaurant further away and said he would meet us there in fifteen minutes.

In contrast to Mrs. Wessinger's surprising calmness, I was wishing I could just shrink down to nothing and disappear. Expecting her to handle the discussion, I was shocked when she suggested that Hugh and I find somewhere private to go and discuss our financial plan together. She knew what he had done to me! How could she so casually suggest such a thing?

When I told her I was afraid to go anywhere alone with him and not to make me leave the restaurant, she said, "Don't be silly. He won't do any thing knowing I'm waiting for you to return. Go ahead. You'll be fine."

Reluctantly, I got into Hugh's sports car. To think I had really known him only a few hours. He could take me anywhere in such a big city. Before I knew it, we were pulling into a remote area. Instinctively, I made a mental note of every detail of the area, in case I needed to make a police report. Trees lined the empty blacktopped parking lot. There were no buildings, no other cars, just trees and asphalt. My nerves were taught, expectant.

Hugh reached over and tried to kiss me. Screaming, I jumped out of the car. "You will never touch me again! Take me back to the restaurant now! It's all your fault I am in this situation."

If looks could kill, I would have been dead. He began pointing his finger and yelling at me, "If you are looking to shake me down for money, just forget it. Tomorrow I'm going to court because of back payments I owe for my sons Scott and Jeffrey. I'm fighting that one. My wife's remarried, and I don't think I should have to pay. If I lose, and I probably will, I won't have any money for you. Besides, I have another wife now and our child to support. This car you probably think is mine, isn't. It's my fathers. He owns the car dealership. So expect nothing from me. I have nothing! Leave me alone!"

He must have been having dinner with his family when he was late for our date. Now I was really scared. "Take me back to the restaurant now," I insisted. Sliding back into the car, I prayed he would obey my command. Slowly, the car moved forward. I sat leaning close to the door, ready in case I needed to make a quick escape. We drove in stiff silence. As soon as the car pulled over in front of the restaurant, I jumped out. Loose gravel scattered off the back tires as he sped away - his answer to the entire matter.

Finding Mrs. Wessinger waiting at a table, I confronted her with what happened. How could she have let me be alone with him! She reassured me that she would take care of everything.

From then on, all the checks I received were signed by his attorney. If checks were late, Mrs. Wessinger took care of it. I never saw Hugh again.

In June, I received my first check in the amount of $125.00, just enough to pay the rent and buy some groceries. The chili I made on Saturday had to last the whole week. Eating in a restaurant was out of the question. Even if I had the money, I would have felt too ashamed. There was little to do with my time, and I was bored. The baby was due mid October.

* * * * * * * *

Trying to be as inconspicuous as possible, I slipped into the vinyl covered, kitchen table-type chair, astonished that I was in a public clinic. It felt degrading. Public clinics were for the poor, not for me with my upper middle class background. The large room was filled with people who were either reading or talking with each other. Most seemed very familiar with the place.

The intake worker, a Mrs. Johnson, asked all the typical questions. As she ran through each one: name, address, phone, employment, I dreaded the one coming up that I never could answer -my date and place of birth. I never could decide whether to put the place where I was found or the place where I grew up.

After an interminable hour's wait, the drill sergeant at the reception desk boomed out, "Mrs. Miller, you are next!" As she led me to the examining room, she confronted me about waiting so long to be checked. "For heaven's sake, you are five months. Now listen carefully," she continued. "There are two things I am going to stress. At this hospital, you have to pay your bills on time and never be late for an appointment."

Not bothering to explain to her that I had already been to a doctor, I promised to do everything she said.

The examining room was like a tiny wooden box. The bench for sitting was only large enough to accommodate my self and my purse. Feeling claustrophobic, I left the curtain open. Not having been told otherwise, I kept my clothes on, though I did notice a hook for hanging them.

In my humiliation, I felt this must be my penance for having a baby out of wedlock. It was a long cry from the way I was raised. Most of our family's friends were doctors or dentists. In fact, my own doctor had lived across the street and often made house calls. I thought of my father's comforting office, the scattered magazines I used to straighten and the happy hours I spent in the yard just outside his window.

The surprising youth of the doctor who hurried into see me, only a few years older than myself, left me feeling uncomfortable. After a quick check, he handed me pink and blue prenatal vitamins and said all was going according to schedule. Pink and blue - girl or boy. Everything still seemed so unreal.

* * * * * * * *

Hiding away in my basement apartment, I felt like I was in prison. My only outings were to the clinic. There was no money for anything else. Television was my only company, and, for the first time in my life, I became a baseball fan. As I watched TV, sitting on the dark mohair couch, I did crossstitching. Often I found myself having to soothe my stomach when the baby kicked too hard. But if any maternal feelings came over me, I squelched them. I didn't think I had the right to such feelings. They felt illegal. The baby seemed healthy from the way it was moving, and for that I was pleased.

Finally tired of lying to my parents about all the flights I was taking, I wrote them a letter explaining everything. As I wrote, I felt acutely that I had failed them. I was indeed a bad seed.

The next thing I knew, my father was knocking at the door. As soon as he read my letter, he closed his practice and drove ten hours to get to me. Never once did he criticize me. He was just there. His kindness was a gift that helped me get through the rest.

My mother was next to arrive, flying for the first time. She wanted to meet Mrs. Wessinger, so lunch was arranged. Mrs. Wessinger also invited Hugh's attorney.

In the midst of our socializing, mother announced in a voice that demanded attention, "I have only one wish for Sally's child. I pray it goes to a good Christian family." Smiling, she continued, "Of course, a good Lutheran home would be even better."

As my mother and Mrs. Wessinger huddled together over the possibility, I had to wonder how important religion really was in the realm of things. A good loving home would be the best request. But, I didn't feel I had a say in the matter. I just had a "condition," one that was just a big mistake, one that needed to be taken care of in the proper Christian way.

But then my mother shocked me. She offered to take care of my baby as her own. Mrs. Wessinger seemed even more astonished than I was. Quickly, she convinced mother that such a thing would cause commotion in her community and her church. It was just not a workable idea, given the society we live in.

As they continued the discussion, Hugh's attorney leaned over to me and smirked, "What's the big deal? You know you enjoyed the sex."

"You pig," I responded coldly, and fled outside to wait for the others. If he had no understanding, who did? That's what everyone would think. Now, I completely understood why my secret was so necessary.

* * * * * * * *

Never before a baseball fan, I became swept up in the World Series. The Brooklyn Dodgers were playing the Chicago White Sox. I don't remember who I was rooting for, but I am sure it was whoever was the underdog. During the deciding game, I was seized by what seemed like a very bad stomach cramp. Then another came along. And another. Then came a few more. I had to grab a hold of the back of the chair for support. What was I to do now?

The first thing that came to mind was an episode of I Love Lucy. When Lucy announced it was time to go to the hospital, her family and friends grabbed the suitcase, one that had been packed and ready for weeks, and walked out the door leaving Lucy behind.

Not knowing if the baby might come any minute, I called a taxi. Upon hearing the horn honking, I picked up my suitcase and calmly walked outside. "Woman's Hospital, please," I said to the driver.

Nervous that he might be the one to deliver the baby, the driver kept peering over his shoulder making chitchat. I did not feel like talking and ignored him. Relieved to be pulling up to the hospital with no incident, the driver asked, "Will someone be meeting you here?" He was concerned.

"No," I responded, paying my fare and feeling defeated. "I am alone."

At first there was a flurry of activity. As soon as I had changed into my hospital gown, I was given an exam. Another nurse entered my room with a pan of soapy water and a razor to prep me. Next came the enema. And then came the waiting.

The wall clock never seemed to be moving. I had no idea what to expect. Lying in bed, I took in everything about the room. White tiles covered the walls and created a cold, sterile feeling. A morgue was probably cheerier.

To pass the time, I played tic tac toe on the square celetex tiles on the ceiling after having already counted them over and over. Why was labor taking so long? I was left all alone except for the times the doctors stopped by to check on my progress. No one lingered to keep me company, not even for a moment. At some point, I was given something to help me sleep.

Twenty-nine hours later, in a drugged-out state, I felt my bed being pushed out of the room and down the hall to another room that looked just like the one I had left. As I was lifted onto a hard examining table, I noticed the large, almost blinding overhead light above me. Everywhere chrome was reflecting the green scrubs of the attendants. With the mask covering his face, it was impossible to tell if this was my doctor from the clinic.

Then, suddenly and unexpectedly, a brown rubber mask was placed over my nose and mouth and everything went blank.

When I awoke, I was still in the delivery room. Instinctively, my hands felt my stomach. It was now empty of my baby. Only loose skin was left to remind me.

The first question out of my mouth was, "Is my baby black?" Not knowing my background and remembering such a gene could skip a generation, I was curious.

The nurse commented coldly to the doctor, "She must still be drugged. She doesn't know what she's saying."

"I'm not drugged," I defended myself. "I'm adopted, and I don't know my past."

"No, it is white," the nurse crisply responded, as if she would expect such a question to come from a woman having a baby out of wedlock.

I felt so cheap.

Void of my child, lying there in a groggy heap with everyone around me busy doing something - tugging at my insides, caring for the baby, chatting with the strange doctor – it seemed I was insignificant, blank, dull and most of all empty.

Back in my room, I was again left all alone and instructed the door must always remain shut. Vaguely aware of nurses coming in and out of my room, I turned my back on the forbidden door.

Later, when I was feeling less groggy, I begged the nurses to tell me anything about my baby. Was it a boy or a girl? How much did it weigh? My questions were ignored.

My constant crying, begging and pleading finally softened one nurse. "You had a girl," she told me, as she hurried out of the room. "Now don't ask me anything else. I'm not allowed to give you any information."

A girl! I had a baby girl! For a moment I was ecstatic. A girl. But I needed to know more. I needed to know everything about her. Does she have any hair? How long is she? A million questions. But all my inquiries fell on deaf ears.

Each time feeding time came around, I had to cover my ears to block out the babies' cries. In silence I screamed, "I want to feed my baby, too!" I had been told I wouldn't get emotionally attached, but they were so wrong. My emotions were over-whelming. All I wanted was to see my baby - now!

But it was hospital policy not to allow mothers who weren't taking their babies home to see them. "It is better this way," one nurse explained to me. "Seeing the baby will only cause you more pain."

Emotionally dead, as if I had just had surgery to remove all feeling, I curled up in a fetal position and kept quiet from then on. I never once gave a thought to either of my mothers.

*   *   *   *   *   *   *   *

The day before I was to be discharged, Mrs. Wessinger arrived with a portable baby carrier. I could not believe she could be so insensitive. Couldn't she have waited? Why did she have to bring it into my room?

Sliding a chair up to my bed, she opened her brief case and pulled out some legal forms. Peering over her pile of papers, she asked, in her best business-like manner, "What do you want to name the baby?"

Her question caught me completely unaware. "No one told me I was allowed to name my baby. You told me not to get attached, or it would make everything harder. I didn't dare give a thought to naming her. Why didn't you tell me?"

Without acknowledging one word I said, she explained, "Well I need one for the birth certificate." Pointing to one of the lines, she went on, "I have to fill out these papers."

As I stared at the baby carrier, my mind rushed to think of a name. None came. Then, all of a sudden, I heard myself say, "Bambi Lynn Miller." Where in the world had that name come from?

Dismayed, Mrs. Wessinger asked me if I really wanted to give my baby that name. Why did she care? The new parents would change it anyway.

"Yes, I am naming her Bambi, because in the Disney story Bambi's mother died, and right now I feel dead, too."

*   *   *   *   *   *   *   *

My friend, Lee, picked me up at the hospital. I remember that. But, I don't remember actually walking out through the doors into the sunlight without my baby. All I had with me to remind me of the birth of my child was the pad to catch the blood and my full and aching breasts. My arms were empty, and so was my heart.

Later that day, I found myself walking along railroad tracks, feeling blue and very much alone. All the advice I had been given about why it was best to give my baby up was running through my head. None of it made any sense now. The pain was so unbearable, I considered throwing myself in front of the next train. Instead, I shrugged my shoulders and turned back towards my little basement apartment. I was not even strong enough to kill myself.

* * * * * * * *

I was still feeling foggy and disconnected when, three days later, Mrs. Wessinger arrived to take me to Children's Home Society to sign the final relinquishment papers. It was the day I had dreaded.

While she chatted away, I gazed out the window, my thoughts frozen. We pulled up to a building, formerly a mansion. Reluctantly, I followed Mrs. Wessinger up to the large porch, counting each step along the way, my eyes fixated on the worn brass knobs of the double doors. Each door framed an oblong piece of beveled glass. The paint was peeling.

Mrs. Wessinger lead the way inside, her brief case swinging powerfully in sync with her stride. "We are here for our appointment," she announced to the receptionist.

The room grew suddenly quiet. The receptionist began typing some important looking papers. With a strange detachment, as if viewing everything through a camera's lens, I scanned the room imagining it when it had been a home. The camera zoomed to the double doors and lingered there. If I ran, where would I go?

The sound of papers being cranked out of the typewriter brought my attention back to the reception desk. The secretary needed help. A voice answered from what must have been the original dining room. We were silent as we waited. My feet were tracing circles on the floor.

The receptionist was saying, "Now stand here, Sally. Witness, you stand next to Mrs. Wessinger. Is every one ready."

It was as if someone were orchestrating a play for little kids. But, now I had to play the role of my life.

My heart was beating so loudly, I could not hear the words she read. My feet were suddenly made of lead.

Bristling with efficiency, the receptionist told me to, "Sign here."

I hesitated.

I became aware of Mrs. Wessinger and the witness moving closer to me. They pointed to where I needed to sign, as if I didn't know, insisting.

Still, I hesitated.

They tried to convince me I was doing the right thing. They seemed nervous and anxious as they talked.

Still, I hesitated. But time had really run out. I saw no other option.

And so I signed, and with my signature, a part of me died.

CHAPTER THREE

Candles in my mother's tall Sterling silver candelabras illuminated the faces of the ladies, members of her circle group from church, who were gathered around the lace-covered dining room table catching up with all the news since their last meeting. My dad and Uncle Jacob had just brought me home, and mother asked me if I would help her serve. We were pretending that everything was normal, as if I hadn't even been gone. I was happy to oblige. Trying not to interrupt their conversation, I slid a plate filled with homemade coconut cake and mounds of vanilla ice cream before each one.

But, then I felt something wet and realized to my horror that the front of my shirt was soaked from the milk that had suddenly leaked from my breasts. Quickly excusing myself, I ran upstairs and threw myself across the bed. My sobs were primal. I was certain my baby girl needed me.

Between my sobs, I could hear the laughter of the women downstairs. Life would go on for them. Mine was standing still. But the damage was done, and there was nothing I could do about it now. Over the next days, I began the process of neatly tucking away all my feelings and memories into a place deep inside that I would never have to visit.

But back at work, nothing felt the same as before, and trying to act as if nothing happened was proving difficult. I was so different from who I used to be.

"Your daughter is beautiful! She has big eyes like yours," a senior member of the ground crew casually yelled over to me one day out of the blue. "We are foster parents, and she is at our house."

I almost died. The hiding, the secrecy had all been in vain! Everyone must know. Embarrassed now, I just knew he would tell everyone. I felt raw. By ignoring his comments, I hoped he would see my distress and get the hint to keep quiet. But, why was my daughter in foster care? Why wasn't she in her new home as I was led to believe would happen?

As I stood in the aisle of the plane, feeling like the whore my mother always used to call me, I wondered if it was visible to others that I had just had a child.

If I thought of trying to see my little baby girl, it was only for a second. My spirit was too broken to believe I could.

* * * * * * * *

Thirteen months later, fate gathered together three unlikely passengers and again my life changed. This time it was for the better.

Because of bad weather, a businessman named Ross, who usually flew his own private plane, booked a commercial flight instead. Dorothy, a frequent flier and student from the Lansing School for the Blind, was unable to book her usual direct flight because of the heavy traffic for Thanksgiving, and instead boarded our plane. It was a sick child, who suddenly threw up all over himself and the seat of the plane that brought us all together.

Cleaning up after the child as best I could, I wished out loud for a brush to clean the ribbed material of the seat. Overhearing my wish, Ross produced an old toothbrush for me to use and we began talking. As we flew over Lake Michigan, Ross pointed out where his cabin cruiser was docked. Thinking boating would be fun, especially with such a nice man, I concocted a plan.

Dorothy was going to need help getting to her connection when we landed in Green Bay, so I asked Ross if he would mind assisting her. When he said he didn't, I insisted he phone me at home to let me know that Dorothy was delivered safely, as she was a very special passenger to all of us. His report back to me led to more phone calls, and soon we were dating.

When I realized our relationship was really getting serious, I told Ross about my daughter. Better to know if it made a difference to him now rather than later. We became engaged after he acknowledged my daughter's importance. But there was one big problem - Ross was Jewish.

My mother, reminding me of the confirmation vows she picked out for me to say from John 3:16, "For God so loved the world that he gave his only begotten son, that whoever believeth in him should not perish, but have everlasting life," she was certain that marrying a Jew would guarantee my going to hell. She began sending crucifixes in the mail with notes sounding very much like the proverbial Jewish mother: "We took you in and this is the thanks we get?"

Torn between my love for Ross and my loyalty to my parents, I was constantly in tears, when this should have been the happiest time. Seeking guidance, I paid my minister a visit. His comment was, "Who knows what religion God is? If you love this man, then marry him."

But, then who would marry us? The minister from our family's church insisted Ross would need to join the Lutheran church. His rabbi said I needed to convert. On August 11, 1961, we settled for a beautiful wedding officiated by the Justice of the Peace.

Within a few weeks, I was pregnant with our first son, Jay. After Jay was born, we sold the boat to the doctor that delivered him. I had become gripped with a fear of slipping and falling into the water with the baby. Three years later, another son, Kiley, came along. Four years later, Daniel was born. For the first time I was with family I was connected to by blood. Bound and determined to be the best mother I could be, I would find myself wandering into their rooms just to stare, and to make sure they did not go away.

My life was packed with activities, so that I rarely had a moment to reflect. I became an energetic volunteer, converted to Judaism and became a religious leader. In fact, I became president of every organization I joined. I became a passionate volunteer advocate for patients' rights in the mental health field.

Yet, at rare moments, I would find myself asking, "Who am I? Why do I always feel so depressed?" But I wouldn't let myself linger long with such questions. I just played all my roles correctly.

A series of events made survival a running theme in my life. First, our house burned down and, after it was rebuilt, it got flooded. Besides the usual kid's emergencies, I had to have major surgery and Kiley almost died in a motorcycle accident. Daniel became an alcoholic. I was certain he must have inherited the tendency from my side, but how could I know? We fought hard for him and he became clean and sober. Through it all, I remained strong.

But then during Friday services at temple one evening, while sitting with the choir, tears I did not understand began streaming down my cheeks, as loved ones lost in the Holocaust were remembered. I was a convert and knew no one lost to the Holocaust. My tears embarrassed me, and I quickly got myself back under control. But, perhaps my mother was Jewish?

*   *   *   *   *   *   *   *

One August morning in 1984, while sipping coffee and reading the newspaper, a photo grabbed my attention. A woman was standing inside the Chicago bus station in the exact same spot where she had been left as an infant years before. The article went on to say the woman was looking for her mother. Feeling a sudden kinship, I was compelled to write the woman. In her reply, she suggested I join a search and support organization called ALMA, the Adoptees' Liberation Movement Association. My search had finally begun.

*   *   *   *   *   *   *   *

My Aunt Rachel used to tell a particular story over and over again about how she just knew her minister and his wife were my parents. The wife apparently looked just like me. "I'll bet he was in the seminary when your mother became pregnant, and since they weren't married they had to give you away!"

My aunt's suspicions, confirmed in her mind, always told me, "The night we were having a meeting at our house about the newly revised standard version of the Bible, which everyone was up in arms about, your adoptive parents arrived. Acting very skittish, the minister, a Mr. Senft, left quickly, suddenly saying he had another appointment. Why would he suddenly have to leave, unless he was afraid of facing your adoptive parents?"

This bit of family lore being all I had to go on at this point, and wanting so much to find my mother, I flew from my home in California to my hometown. I would pay the Senft family a visit. My parents agreed to go with me. Before we left, my mother changed her outfit three times, "just in case it was them."

My heart was pounding so fast, as my dad pulled up to the Senft house, that I was certain my shirt was visibly moving to its rhythm. Mustering all my courage, I knocked on the door. No answer. No response to the doorbell either. Fiddling with the doorknob, I was surprised to discover it was unlocked. Peaking my head inside, I called out, "Hello, hello. Anyone home?" Still there was no answer. Since the door was unlocked, they couldn't be far or gone for long. I wanted to wait. Dad read the paper while Mom and I chatted, but then decided it was best to return home. Protesting, I suggested we go to lunch and then try again.

Still there was no one home, even after another long wait. Before we left, I wrote a note and slipped it through the open door. "I think you are my birth father, and I am disappointed I didn't get a chance to meet you. Here is my name and address. Please contact me.

A few weeks later, a letter arrived from the minister stating that he was not my father, but he did have adopted grandchildren. He offered to contact the Senft family who had found me. Though they shared the same last name, they weren't related.

Then one day, a letter arrived from Janet Senft Booz. She was elected spokesperson for the family, she said, because she was the one who found me in the paper bag. Her letter revealed no new information. Despite the fact that it all seemed so unreal still, I found my interest in searching was suddenly intensified.

After attending an ALMA meeting, I was armed with a list of things to do. I contacted the Pennsylvania Department of Public Welfare Office of Children, Youth and Family Services to find out from them which agency had handled my adoption, and to request all non-identifying information in my file. They were not allowed to pass along any information that would lead to the direct identification of who my parents were.

Next, I wrote to the Court of Common Pleas for a copy of the Petition to Adopt and Final Decree.

While waiting for those responses, I sent a certified letter with a signed return receipt request to the York Hospital for the records of my six-week stay there. I also wrote the State Police, hoping they had a record of the night I was found, and requested a copy of my long form birth certificate from the State of Pennsylvania.

The signed receipt from the hospital was returned, but no records ever arrived. Child and Family Services never acknowledged my request for non-identifying information and, after being informed by the Court of Common Pleas that my records were sealed, I didn't even bother contacting Child and Family Services again. The State Police did let me know that records over twenty-five years old were automatically purged from their files. Months of waiting and there was not a shred of information to help me. I was feeling very discouraged.

"Foundlings have the hardest time finding their loved ones, because they have no paper trail to follow," the ALMA support group leader informed me at the next meeting I attended. She suggested I run an ad in the local newspaper where I had been found. The ad produced nothing.

After months of searching and not the slightest lead, I felt it was time to give it up. In the next five years, both of my adoptive parents died, and I felt like an orphan again. Everyone but me was happy when the family house sold. For forty-five years, that house had been my safety net, my port in the storm. Where was I to return to now?

* * * * * * * *

New Years Eve morning, 1994, I was awakened with a start when a voice way deep inside me said, "This is the year you will search for your mom." Ten years before searching proved futile, so why this year? And whose voice was this? Never before had I ever heard "voices." But, somehow I knew to pay attention. And so, in the quiet of those early morning hours, I made the commitment to try once again. I would give it a year, but no more.

Just a short time later, Los Angeles was struck by an earthquake, and I was rocked to my senses. One never knows what will happen tomorrow, or if there will even be a tomorrow. My commitment was strengthened, and I just knew I was going to be successful.

Making a commitment was like setting the Universe in motion. A week after the quake, the Russian interpreter for my husband's business called asking for a favor. Could his friend come to our house to wash and bleach her hair? Because of the earthquake, the water in her faucets was coming out brown. I was glad to be of help.

His friend Vicki, arrived carrying a large collection of holistic medicines. Her hair did need drastic attention. Over the course of her stay, Vicki revealed she was psychic, but she only used her gift to help others medically.

Not having much experience, but a lot of curiosity about psychics, I pondered about whether to trouble her by asking what she thought my nationality was. Finally, I screwed up my courage and told her I was adopted and don't know my past.

Lifting her head from out of the sink, and wrapping her hair up in a towel, Vicki just stared at me. "Well, do you have a list of all the countries in the world?" she asked.

My mind went blank. I asked her where I would get such a list. She suggested I look up "world" in the encyclopedia.

Pulling the book off the shelf, I opened it to "Countries of the World" and left the list on the dining room table. Vicki went outside where her mother was reading and watching their dog and, with her help, determined my nationality by psychic kinestheseology. Vicki held her arm out to her side and asked a question and then her mother would try to push her arm down. If Vicki's muscles could resist her mother's pressure, the answer was yes.

Walking back into the house, still in a slight trance state, Vicki headed for the opened encyclopedia. Calmly and with certainty she said, "Your mother is three quarters Welsh and one quarter English. Your father is three quarters Irish and one quarter German.

Appearing to have forgotten something, she headed back outside repeating the muscle testing with her mother. Returning she commented, "Something was bothering me. That is why I went back outside. Your father is one quarter Austrian, not German."

This was the closest I had come to knowing anything about my heritage. But, whether it was true or not, I had no way of proving on the physical plane of reality. My search continued.

Acting on advice from ALMA searchers, I also decided to get as much press coverage as possible, which would hopefully lead to some information. Within a few weeks, I found six newspapers willing to run my story. I also asked my brother to check the family safe. But there was nothing in there that I didn't already know.

The morning of my fifty-fifth birthday, one newspaper in York, Pennsylvania called, and after a lengthy interview, informed me that my story would run in their Sunday edition, coming out the very next morning. As I hung up the phone, I realized this was the very same paper that had run my original foundling story in 1939!

The story produced one result. Alfretta, the student nurse who had taken care of me while I was in the hospital and had named me Judy, wrote me a letter. In the letter, she told me all that she remembered of our time together. Apparently, I had become the mascot for their graduating class. But, there were no clues in her letter to help my search along.

Then I heard from my hometown newspaper. They wanted to do my story and at first I was excited. But then I panicked. I had never talked about being adopted with any of my friends, though I assumed they all knew. Imagining their reaction brought me to unexpected and puzzling tears.

The story ran on the front page, which shocked me. It was given equal billing with former President Richard Nixon's funeral.

Not a single clue came from that article, either. But I did hear from an amateur genealogist offering her services investigating family trees. Obviously, the woman did not have any idea about what it meant to be adopted and be without hope of ever discovering one's ancestral heritage. In school, to fulfill the assignment, I used my adoptive family's tree. But, after I got credit for the assignment, I had dumped it in the trash.

When I fantasized about my family tree, which was often, I would imagine a unique tree standing out in a beautiful meadow, one like near Pine Grove Lake, an area that I loved in Pennsylvania. While its branches swayed in a soft breeze like the other trees, my tree would stand out because of the large gash on its trunk where an important branch had been severed. Sap would be dripping like tears from its wound, the place along the trunk from which I had been torn, the amputation of me. The outstretched branches of my tree would be all the relatives I was waiting to embrace.

* * * * * * * *

I received another letter from Janet Senft Booz, and in this one there were clues. Enclosed with Janet's letter was a long article that I had never seen about my discovery. For years, the article had hung framed on the wall over the Senft family radio.

There I was - Miss "X" they called me in the article. A nurse was holding me and I was crying. My little feet were poking out from the blanket I was wrapped in. It was the first picture of myself as a baby that I remembered seeing. My parents must not have had a camera when I was young. Taking all the information in, I was overwhelmed with emotion.

The article provided wonderful details that promised hope with my search, including the name of the manufacturer of the brown paper bag I was found in - C. E. Stevens, Famous Paper Bags.

As I read the words, my mother became a little more real to me. Before leaving me on the porch, she had clothed me in a blue trimmed white dress, pinned closed with a gold safety pin, and hand knitted booties, cap and jacket. Had she knitted them herself? She had wrapped me in two, used blue and white baby blankets decorated with Scotty dogs and included a four-ounce bottle of milk, the kind with a transparent amber nipple connected to a black base. A police description of the car was given:

> The car was either a blue or black sedan, probably a Plymouth. A man and a woman were in the car. The man was of stocky build and the woman was about five feet six inches tall and of slender build. The woman was seen by passing motorists to leave the car about 7:20 o'clock last evening and approach the Senft home. Her mission, of course, was not known by those who saw her.

Apparently, there was an indelible ink mark on my leg, just above the right knee. Was this for my mother to be able to track whether I had been found? Had she written a note and thought better of it, some ink from the pen accidentally getting on my leg as she wrote hastily in the car?

For some reason, the police had judged me to be of Italian parentage - not at all what the psychic had picked up.

Pursuing the additional clues was an exercise in futility. Oddly, the State of Maryland had no records of foundlings for either 1938 or 1939. The records for those years were missing somehow. I found myself not trusting that she looked hard enough. Curious just for herself, a worker in Pennsylvania, learning there was no record of my birth there, double-checked. Then she called me out of the blue one Saturday morning to confirm my suspicions.

My birth was probably never registered as neither Maryland nor Pennsylvania had any record that came close to matching my story.

It had taken until I was five and a half to even get my fake birth certificate. All dressed up for my first day of school, I could barely contain my excitement. As I stood at the table with my mother, I sensed trouble and heard the ladies say, "Yes, we know you are a teacher Mrs. Miller, but we can't bend the rules. A birth certificate is necessary to enroll your daughter in school." Of course, I had no idea of the significance then. As we quickly left the building, my mother kept saying over and over, "I am so sorry. I am so sorry." I had no idea what she was sorry about.

Depositing me back home, my mother dashed off to Harrisburg, and explained the problem to Vital Records. They issued her a certificate with made up information, since no one knew my real birth date or place of birth. Five and a half years after I was born, I finally became legitimized – sort of.

Getting my identifying information from the agency through the court system was easy for a rather twisted reason. Even though I was fifty-six years old, I was only entitled to the records because my parents were deceased and therefore were no longer considered clients. All I had to do was send them a copy of their death certificates. But the only new information I gleaned was that my parents petitioned the court to adopt Baby "X" on February 1, 1940, nearly one year from the day I was found.

* * * * * * * *

Relaxing by our pool one day and leafing through the mail, I discovered a brochure for an adoption conference to be held in New York City in the fall. The organization was the Council for Equal Rights in Adoption (CERA).

Sessions for adoptees, birth parents, adopted parents and mental health professionals included titles such as: "But I Never Had Boundaries", "How Can I Just Be Me?" and "Outgrowing (Some) of the Pain."

For the first time, I realized that I might have to begin to deal with my issues of being a birth mother, as well as my adoptee issues. But, if I registered as both, would they put that on my convention badge, and would everyone then think of me as a loose woman? It was bad enough being adopted, but to be a birth mother, too? I decided to just go as an adoptee.

But, as I checked off the sessions I wanted, completed my registration form and wrote out the check, I found myself marking both adoptee and birth parent boxes. Quickly stuffing everything into the envelope provided, I rushed to the post office before I could change my mind. For the first time in thirty-five years, I admitted to being a birth mother.

* * * * * * * *

Searching with so much effort producing few results. I grew depressed. At least, that is what I attributed my depression to, my reason for not wanting to go anywhere. I lost my sense of self and I was floating, having no direction. My friend Jeannette called wondering if I might want to visit a psychic with her for a reading. Once already, I had accompanied Jeannette to the same psychic after her husband had died, and I knew she was good. Perhaps the psychic could shed some light on my background.

"You are a writer or a composer," was the first thing she said to me as I sat down for my reading. "In fact you have written a cookbook. You just don't know what to do with it." She certainly had my attention. What she said was true.

Then she asked me if I had a daughter. I answered, "No." But she was insistent. In all innocence, I suggested she could be referring to my granddaughter, my son Kiley's daughter. My denial was so deep that I had not connected her question with my truth.

Tears began to flow as I heard her say toward the end of the reading that both my biological parents were dead. To console me she said, "You are very fortunate you came into this life. Look at the wonderful children you have. You have helped a lot of people.

"Your mother was old when she died," she went on. "Her hair was gray. It looks like she had something wrong in the throat area, had alcoholism or something that took her."

My adoptive mother had died of throat problems.

"She wasn't who she wanted to be and spent her whole life that way."

I knew she could not be talking about my adoptive mother now.

"Since you were born, she thought about you every birthday and times in between. Her belief was giving you away was one of the good things she did in her life - providing you with a good home."

That seemed true.

"You couldn't have lived with her. She was young and just couldn't handle you. It was the best thing, though she could have handled it a better way. But, she didn't want any criticism. She may not have even known the father, but he is gone never-the-less. She didn't want to get arrested. She had a hard enough time taking care of herself.

"Not knowing them is a tragedy for you, and for her. Look at the beautiful, wonderful child she never got to know. But you can talk to them on "the other side," and you may get an answer back, even if you don't know their names. Just thank them for bringing you into this world. The world is a better place for you being here. Just ask your children, especially your husband. Bless their hearts, they provided you with a chance."

By now, I was crying profusely. "She is the one whose heart aches even more than yours, because she never got to know you. No mother can give birth without it making a huge difference in her life. I get a name - Irene. I get the name, Patrick, for the man. It doesn't seem like he knew he was a father. She was a very brave person considering what she had to go through. I certainly would not castigate her at all."

"What is my nationality?" I always needed to ask that.

She said Irish, some Scandinavian, Northern Europe, maybe Scotch. "A nice mixture."

The psychic at my house told me pretty much the same. Could my birth family be Catholic, I wondered?

But, perhaps both psychics were referring to my father. My mother, according to the police report in the newspaper article, had looked Italian.

Finally, I just had to ask her if she could tell when my birthday was.

"Let's find a birthday for you. February 5 comes to me."

That was the day I was found, I told her. Looking deeper, she said my birthday was January 18. But, that didn't compute with my story. My parents first saw me in the hospital on February 9, and I was supposed to be two weeks old then. My birthday should be somewhere between the twenty-third and twenty-ninth of January, making me an Aquarian, not a Capricorn. Who could I believe?

As I waited for my friend's reading to be over, I could not let myself believe my parents were dead. My mother was an alcoholic? Could the psychic be right? In my fantasies growing up, I always saw my parents sitting up to the bar in a lovely, upscale establishment, maybe somewhere in New York City. The bar had richly ornate wood throughout. I would stand for hours, observing through the beveled glass doors, my parents chatting and laughing together. Always, I hoped and prayed they would turn around so I could see their faces. But they never did.

CHAPTER FOUR

Inside the local fire hall, not far from where I was found, eighty members of the Senft clan gathered for a family reunion. As I rushed in, late after getting lost, I searched the sea of strange faces for the third person to link me with this family. A Senft family found me, and the minister and his wife who looked like me, who my aunt suspected were my real parents, were also Senfts. Now Geraldine Senft Thomas, who contacted me after seeing my story in a newspaper, had invited me here, certain we were related. As I searched the room for her, I wondered if this new Senft did indeed look like me as she claimed.

After apologizing for being so late, I sat down next to Geraldine and her daughter in the seat they had been saving. It was exciting meeting Geraldine. She was warm and friendly, just as I had expected. After dinner, I wanted to stand up and thank them all for the role the Senft family had played in my life. But my heart was racing too fast and the lump in my throat would not go away. So, I kept silent.

The whole time, I searched every face for a hint of resemblance. Perusing the long table full of Senft family artifacts, I studied photographs of those not in attendance hoping to find something to link me with them. In awe, I poured through a book, the size of a large novel, chronicling the history of the Senft clan. The first Senft, John Philip, had arrived in Philadelphia on September 16, 1751 and settled close by where I had been found. But, never having had any blood relatives to mirror me, how would I know if I were looking at someone I was related to?

The happy occasion was taking its toll, however. Being surrounded by such a huge clan made the void of not knowing my own history acutely painful. I left the reunion feeling very much out of step with life.

* * * * * * * *

September had become a month of meeting strangers with whom I had much in common. My next stop was the adoption convention in New York City. Frightened to be going to the city by myself, I gathered strength from knowing it was something I needed to do. Little did I know the impact it would have on my life.

Surrounded by three hundred people from all walks of life representing birth parents, adoptees, adopted parents and professionals, I felt more connected than I had in a very long time, if ever. We all shared similar feelings and understood each other's stories at the deepest levels. As I observed the birth mothers, I discovered my relief at the fact that they all looked normal. I guess I had expected some to look like "low lifes," and realized that that was just a projection of how I might feel about myself in some ways, or how my mother had felt about me at times.

Pinning on my badge, I was happy I had not been labeled "birth mother," or "adoptee." As I was getting deeper into my search, I was finding myself being bantered back and forth emotionally between my role as a birth mother and my role as an adoptee. My idea about what each role meant to me was constantly changing, causing me to feel I really didn't know life at all.

As I anticipated searching for my daughter, I thought that being adopted would help me understand my daughter's feelings. But the trauma of relinquishing her clouded my perceptions. It was difficult to sort out what grieving mode

I was in at times. Was I grieving the loss of my daughter or the loss of my mother? Was the pain I was feeling from my original abandonment, or from being apart from my daughter? One often triggered the other, and as I continued to search, the pounding in my head, from my struggle to understand the sometimes deep dark pit holes of despair, became constant. Finding no guidelines, I had begun to write in an attempt to sort myself out. I hoped what I would learn at the conference would help.

In the very first session, the therapist who was also an adoptee talked about boundaries, a term I was embarrassed to realize I had never heard used. Apparently, adoptees do not know how to form boundaries naturally. The workshop leader asked us to form an imaginary boundary around ourselves, in any shape and as wide as we needed. Mine became a two foot square boxing me in.

We were also made aware of our body language. The therapist explained that when adoptees talk about being adopted, their shoulders slump and their breathing becomes shallow. Immediately I reacted thinking, that this idea was crazy, until I realized that I was slumping myself and barely breathing.

The day's sessions left me emotionally drained, and I had to force myself to attend the support group meeting being held afterwards. Dragging my body into the room, I slid into a chair too overwrought to do anything but stare into space. The room hummed with conversations sharing the events of the day until the support group leader spoke.

"Is anyone having a hard time emotionally?" he asked. "Anyone want to share?"

All of a sudden, I found myself the one standing up. What in the world was I doing? Feeling like a volcano about to erupt, I was afraid I wouldn't be able to speak. Then all of a sudden, thirty-five years of secrets were spilled out into the room.

I heard myself say, "Hi, my name is Sally and I am an adoptee and a birth parent." As my words made their way into the ethers of the room, I waited for the inevitable condemnation, especially the part about being a birth mother. None came.

So, I continued, "In the middle of the winter, my birth mother put me in a paper bag and dumped me on a farm house porch. The press called me 'Baby X' - a foundling." My sobs made it almost impossible to continue. Gasping for air, I went on. "When I was nineteen, I got pregnant and had to give my child away. For thirty-five years, I have never told anyone about this, except my husband."

At that moment, I honestly thought I was going to die. Joe Soll, the therapist leading the session, came over and put his arms around me and said, "When our emotions make us feel we are about to die, the brain knows we have had enough and shuts down. It will not allow us to continue having those strong feelings. Not until we can handle them. Remember this when you are feeling overwhelmed. You will be fine."

I needed to know this, because at that moment, the pain and shame I was feeling for allowing myself to get pregnant and being talked into surrendering my child was unbearable. What if my daughter was feeling the same pain? How could I have kept this so deeply buried all these years? To think my children did not know they had a sister. But, my husband had told me not to tell them, as it was all in the past. How could I tell them anyway?

After two days of intensely emotional sessions, it was time to return to my brother's house in Pennsylvania. With only a few hours left before my train departed, I rushed to the bookstore for some last minute purchases. One of the women there said that, given my circumstances, I should consult the psychic who was hired by the convention to help searchers.

The psychic was booked but a kind soul, seeing how rushed I was, offered me her slot. I felt it must be fate and sat down in the seat before Penny, the psychic. As Penny closed her eyes, she said she felt my mother was still alive, that her name could be Mary Teresa Sennet. Did that ring a bell? The name sounded like it could be a nun's. She felt the area where I was left was well chosen.

Then she began talking rapidly. "The car was facing toward the house which was on the right, leading into a small town. The car could have originated from within a hundred mile radius. Mother was seventeen, petite, wearing saddle shoes and socks and a plain dress with a flower print. She had light brown to blond hair. She kissed you on the forehead before leaving you on the porch."

Because her tape recorder had not worked, she asked me to send a picture of the house where I was found that I was going to go see for the first time in a few days. She promised to do another reading from the picture. Thanking her, I rushed to catch my train.

After settling into my seat, I watched the passing scene through the windows of the train and thought about the previous readings I'd had from psychics. Was my mother alive or was she dead? Do I grieve or do I celebrate? Mercifully, my brain finally shut down, and I could not think about one more subject related to adoption.

* * * * * * * *

As excited as I had been about seeing the house where I was left, I found myself pacing my brother's house, crying like a wounded animal and wondering what in the world I was going to do. For the first time, I was meeting Janet Senft, the woman, who as a young girl, was the one to discover me on her family porch. We were to have lunch together first, and then Janet would take me to her family home. My hysteria was unexpected. What if I couldn't make the trip after all these years? Why was I so afraid of seeing the house?

The hour drive through the beautiful tranquil back roads of Pennsylvania calmed me.

After lunch at a restaurant on the outskirts of York, I followed Janet in my rental car to the township of Thomasville to, at last, see "the house." As we headed down the country road, I realized we were going in the very direction the New York psychic said the dark car carrying me had gone.

Janet pulled off the road in front of an empty lot, and I followed. All I saw was a pile of stones from a quarry. Rolling down the window of her car, Janet called out that this was where Farmer Sundy's farm house used to stand. This was where my mother had first intended to leave me. Sundy was the one who provided the police with a description of the car, and the people inside.

Continuing down the highway and crossing over the railroad tracks, Janet's car again pulled over to the side of the road. This had to be the house.

Studying the former Senft family home through the windshield of my car, I realized that I had imagined it differently. The porch was surprisingly small. In my mind it had always been huge, like the porches found on the homes of southern plantations.

Two large windows, reaching almost to the porch floor, were to the left of the front door. A few steps down from the porch the small lawn blended into the busy highway. A gravel driveway, running along the entire right side of the deep house, lead to an unattached garage in the back. The house stood alone in open fields, which looked to be farmland. Wind caused the vegetation to dance and bow, as if welcoming me back. Everything felt surreal.

The wind ripped through my clothes as I got out of my car. As I walked toward Janet, I pulled my jacket tighter around me, and surveyed the whole area. I had the feeling this would not be farmland much longer and was happy I was able to see the farm house as it was when I was left there, before the area became more residential.

Over and over I kept saying to myself, "So this is where I started my journey, out here on this porch all alone."

As we walked up to the house, Janet pointed to the far side of the porch, away from the front door, away from the windows. "I found you over here," she said.

Somehow, I had believed I was placed directly in front of the door, where deliveries are placed. Unanticipated emotions welled up in me. Heat rose up from my gut as I felt sudden rage. How could she have placed me where I could not be immediately seen or heard?

No one responded to the doorbell. Cupping her hands around her eyes, Janet peaked through one of the large front windows and then waved me over.

"This is the front parlor. The house has two. The other one is located behind this one. I was in the second parlor when I heard your cries."

From where I was left on the porch, I must have been crying pretty loudly for Janet to hear me. Then I realized for the first time that Janet had actually saved my life. If she hadn't heard my cries and decided to investigate, I would have died from exposure that cold winter night. My tears, as I hugged and thanked her, were probably as hard as the ones I had cried the night I was found.

Wind from the fast moving trucks caused our bodies to sway as we came down the steps. Pointing to the vacant lot across the street, Janet said, "That was where the man who went with my dad to take you to the hospital lived. A truck ran into his house, destroying it completely."

Finally having talked ourselves out, we hugged goodbye. After Janet drove off, I lingered in front of the house in deep thought. Just knowing my mother had once been in this exact location, I was very reluctant to leave. It was as if I could feel my mother's presence somehow.

At last, I had to go. I said a silent goodbye to my beginnings and to my mother's ghost, and pulled onto the busy highway. My skin hurt, as if I were bleeding from every pore in my body. The pounding of my heart frightened me. Never before had I felt like this. I was so unnerved, in fact, that I thought about having a drink. But it was too early in the day.

Up ahead, I saw a yard sale and pulled over, hoping something so normal might help me feel normal again. But, leafing through the merchandise did nothing to distract my mind that only wanted to go over and over the thoughts of the day. The urge for a drink was so strong. Had I felt this way when I was left alone on the porch as an infant? "Breathe!" I told myself.

All the way back to Carlisle, I felt enormous amounts of energy filling the car, leaving me fighting for my own space. I couldn't wait to get out.

The fall day had turned crisp by the time I arrived. To soothe my bleeding soul, I decided to go for a walk. But first I had to buy something to keep me warm, and stopped at the local stationary store, which catered to the college students, and for some reason bought a Dickinson Law School sweat shirt, probably subconsciously wishing I had more power of the law to open my records.

Walking past all the buildings that held so many memories, my father's dental office, my piano teacher's house, my old home only soothed a bit of my shattered nerves.

Still far from comforted, I went for a therapeutic massage with my sister-in-law, Emily. Unexpectedly, my session became like a magical moment in time, and I was able to let go of so many memories that my body had been holding for a very long time. Released from so much "baggage," I found myself startlingly able to feel the flow of energy between the healer and myself, as we shared our stories. We were on the same wavelength connected intensely with each other. When I got up off the table, I saw a glow radiating from her. Was I seeing an angel? Too embarrassed to say anything, I started getting dressed. When we hugged goodbye, she thanked me for sharing and told me I taught her a lot. I had no idea what she could have learned from me.

Hours later, feeling enveloped in a peace beyond anything I had ever experienced, I suddenly knew without any doubt that I had to find my daughter. The angel had spoken.

* * * * * * * *

When I returned to California, I quickly processed the film and sent pictures of the Senft house to the psychic from the convention. After seeing the house, she sent the tape she had promised.

> Your birth mother wore a dress that had a Peter Pan collar and wore a light coat, one more suitable for wearing in the spring or fall. I feel your placement on the porch was well planned. I don't think this was something that wasn't planned ahead of time.
>
> Your mother had driven many times by this house, searching for just the right place to leave you. The area was chosen because of the good people who lived there. You were left with a lot of love and caring. It was strange, but it was something this poor girl had to do. She did not want to do this, but had no choice. There certainly is a lot of religious connotations around her which leads me to believe her family was very religious, or that she had gone on into the convent, or that someone in her family was in the convent. This was not a random dropping. This was done intentionally and that much planning was done when you were left.
>
> I can not get over how much I get the feeling that this was well planned. You should look into the

> small area, the small community where those people went to church. It has some connection to religion somehow. Maybe a church in another city was involved with the same denomination found in the small town. Where you were placed was investigated and chosen. Your mother would not have abandoned you. She would not have taken you to a stranger's house and put you on the porch. This is the most important thing I am getting. Look towards the big city and look through yearbooks. She lived close enough to keep an eye on you.

Well now, I was totally confused. Racking my brain to think of someone growing up that could have been my mother, I could think of no one. Overwhelmed, having no idea what to believe, I had to set aside the search for my mother and turn instead to the search for my daughter.

* * * * * * * *

The first obstacle in my search for my daughter was caused by the natural memory loss from the trauma of giving her up. Still it was a horror to me. As much as I tried, I could not remember her birthday, an essential piece of information in any search, and I was devastated. The middle of October, 1959 was as close as I could get. Needing guidance, I joined Concerned United Birth Parents (CUB) and began gathering facts following the formula in their search book.

First, I wrote for my hospital records, hoping to discover my daughter's birthday.

Next I wrote the Department of Social Services in Lansing, Michigan asking about what services they had to offer me in my search. They sent me the Parent's Consent/Denial To Release Information to Adoptee form to fill out and send back to be placed in Michigan's Adoption Central Registry. If and when my daughter contacted probate court or the agency that placed her for information, it could then be released. I eagerly filled out the forms and sent them back. I also filled out a form for the International Soundex Reunion Registry, planning to update my scanty information as I received it to increase my odds of a match.

Thus empowered, I got up my nerve to call Michigan Children's Aid Society in Detroit, the agency that handled the adoption and was informed their name had been changed to Child and Family Services and the office had moved to Okemos. In the midst of my frantic-looking doodles, I drew a square and wrote their new number inside it. Then hung up.

My body shook with fear, as I realized I would be calling the same people who had talked me into relinquishing my daughter. However, my need to know overcame my fear, and I dialed the number, feeling like I was doing something illegal.

The voice on the other end was kindly. Mine was timid as I told her I was seeking information about the daughter I had given up for adoption. Embarrassed, I told her I wasn't certain of my daughter's date of birth or if they were even the right agency. She promised to get back to me.

A few days later, the agency called and told me I did indeed have the correct agency. To enable them to access my records and provide non-identifying information, I needed to send sixty dollars. Not knowing what non-identifying information was exactly; I was still excited and quickly sent off my check.

Next, I wrote to Wayne County Juvenile Court requesting a copy of the relinquishment papers. As I searched, I was remembering and I remembered signing papers, though I was never given a copy of anything I had signed. I had to wonder why not?

The first information to arrive was my hospital records. Heart pounding, I slid the information from the manila envelope. As I read the information, it felt like the words were just sliding off my brain as if it were made of Teflon. All that registered was a strangely dawning awareness that, yes, this did happen to me. I did give my child away. It said so right here in black and white.

Quickly flipping through the mass of paperwork, I found my daughter's date of birth. October 27, 1959, a week later than I thought. One day apart from my granddaughter's.

She weighed eight pounds at birth. Wow! No mention was made of her length. She was not released from the hospital until November sixth, because of jaundice. My daughter had jaundice. No one ever told me that!

Feeling suddenly sick, I laid down the thick report. My daughter had been in the hospital for ten days without me, and not with some loving family as I had thought. I could have stolen her back!

My nerves were frayed as I read through the papers and absorbed the truth. I needed time alone to process everything. But instead, when someone called out needing me, I rejoined the family and acted as if everything was normal. This I could do in an instant after so many years of practice.

Later, I found a quiet moment to return to reading the records. Nurses had written notes about me. The day after Bambi's birth one wrote, "The patient seems upset, very nervous. Took her cigarettes to the nurses' station." On the day I named her there was one comment, "Patient quiet." I shoved the hospital report aside, unable to read anymore.

* * * * * * * *

In my emotional state and doing two searches at the same time, I knew I had better be super organized and bought binders for each search and began logging all correspondence.

My friend Joan suggested that, although the Internet probably could not help me find my mother, it may very well lead me to my daughter and offered to help post information for me.

Figuring nothing ventured, nothing gained, I sent away for my daughter's original birth certificate and was surprised to receive it. Now, if I met her, I could give her something she could not ask for herself. But why wasn't the father's name listed?

Then the non-identifying information I had requested arrived. It all fit neatly onto one eight by eleven inch paper.

Child and Family Services of Michigan
Non-identifying Information

Name at birth:	Bambi Lynn Miller
Adoptive father:	(left blank)
Age (at time of adoption):	Late twenties.
Race:	English, German, Dutch, Irish
Religion:	Protestant
Height:	5'11"
Weight:	165 lbs.
Hair:	Medium brown
Complexion:	Medium
Eyes:	Blue
Education:	Associates Degree
Adoptive Mother:	(left blank)
Age (at time of adoption):	Mid twenties
Race:	German, Jewish, Dutch
Religion:	Protestant
Height:	5'6"
Weight:	155 lbs.
Hair:	Medium brown
Complexion:	Fair
Eyes:	Brown
Education:	One year college
Occupation:	Secretary
Health:	Good

Bambi Lynn Miller was born, 10-27-59, at Woman's Hospital in Detroit, Michigan. At birth she weighed 8 lbs. and was 21" in length. She arrived at 4:00 p.m. and was described as a very healthy newborn. She had medium brown hair and a medium to fair complexion. She was placed in her adoptive home at approximately five weeks of age. The adoptive couple had been married approximately four years and Bambi was their first adoptive placement.

At three months, Bambi was described as a beautiful baby with large eyes and a small mouth. Her feeding and sleeping patterns were normal.

At six months, Bambi was adjusting well to her adoptive placement. She was described as having hazel eyes and her facial features were evolving. She liked to smile and was beginning to jabber.

At nine months, she was crawling and had six teeth. She loved to eat and her sleeping patterns were normal. She was described as a very happy and responsive baby.

At twelve months, she was beginning to walk.

Her adoption was confirmed 01/16/61 through the Ingham Probate Court.

* * * * * * * *

Over and over, I read the description for the adoptive mother. She was only a few years older than me. How could she have been a better mother? I could have given my daughter just as good a home, I was certain. My job as a stewardess was a good paying one, the salary the same as teachers. But she was married and I wasn't. I lost my daughter because I wasn't married. It was hard to take in even all these years later.

After I calmed down, I picked the report up again and read the description of my daughter. Her eyes were large and hazel, just like my son Jay's. Imagining her small mouth made my heart ache. They had listed her time of birth wrong. It was actually 4:20 p.m., not 4:00 p.m. I was glad to have the original birth certificate for the correct information.

The adoption was actually finalized the same year and in the same county as was my wedding. This was shocking. All the years I lived in Michigan, my daughter was close by.

My need to know my daughter became the driving force of my life, and at the same time both of my searches slowed to a near standstill. Depressed, tired and just plain obsessed, I wondered if I needed psychological counseling. All my years advocating for mental patients being held against their will helped me to know that technically, at least, I was not crazy. Never had I imagined myself needing such services, so it was difficult to admit I did now. Research at the library produced the name of a therapist specializing in adoption issues, a Dr. Middleman. An appointment was made for the next month when the therapist returned from vacation. Not sure I actually needed help, I could wait a month.

Meanwhile, I continued my search. Contacting a search and support group in Michigan where Bambi was relinquished, I learned of a new state law that provided a confidential intermediary for adoptees and birth parents to contact the person being searched for. There was a nominal fee and I had to petition the court. Although I was accepted to have an intermediary, the law was so new, there was no one trained and no training program was set to begin until April, three months away. Of course, I was not thrilled having to wait, but what choice did I have? Meanwhile, I insisted that the searcher they assign to me be an expert. If I kept a positive attitude, I was sure positive results would follow.

Still, I wondered about my mental health at times. Was I going nuts? Why couldn't I be happy about being adopted as others were? My life was good. My perceived instability must have had another cause.

Desperately looking for answers, I was fortunate to find *Birthmother* by Mary Bloch Jones while browsing the shelves of a bookstore. It said:

> Every loss in life is acknowledged except the relinquishment of your child. If someone dies, there is a funeral. If someone retires, there is a celebration, a gift, something. When losses are socially acceptable, occurring within the basic guidelines of social structure, they evoke emotional support that assists the process of grief and, thus, the progress of affected individuals. However, when losses occur outside its norms, society withholds its mechanisms of comfort from those who grieve.
>
> Society turns its back on birth mothers who have relinquished, denying them the very rituals and tools that might have helped them recover, afterward.

Oblivious to anyone around me, I sank to the floor, the book propped on my lap. Perhaps this was my problem. Could I be grieving?

CHAPTER FIVE

"Your life, Sally, has had many beginnings without any true endings." As I sat talking with the therapist for the first time, I still wondered if I needed to be there. All I wanted was my money's worth and to be fixed immediately, rid finally of this inner turmoil I had lived with all my life. I wanted to tell her to just take it from me. She was telling me I had another layer of problems having been brought up adopted in a family that had their own biological children. Still, as I made another appointment, I wondered if I really needed this kind of help.

But, the layers were begging to be disclosed. While at the library, I found myself pulling a book off the shelf titled, *Strong at the Broken Places: Overcoming the Trauma of Childhood Abuse*. My impulse was to cover the title to hide the feelings of guilt for even thinking I could have been abused. Instead, I should feel grateful my parents took me out of the cold and gave me a good home. Everyone suffers. My life wasn't any harder than other kids' lives, adopted or not. Besides, maybe I wasn't abused. But then I read the section on Post Traumatic Stress Disorder. Trauma is experienced whenever something triggers the memory of an event. The author, Linda Sanford, gave an example that really spoke to me.

> As a child Rita was befriended by a Native American Medicine man who told her to never forget the violence in her family. "He taught me to make a mental snapshot of it, frame it and then put the frame face down. He said it would always be there and when I was ready, I would pick it up, look at it and begin

> dealing with it. I couldn't think clearly or feel fully about the abuse as a child, but now I can look squarely at the trauma.
>
> When you are ready to turn the picture over, memories and feelings begin to reconnect. You REMEMBER with the heart and mind instead of DISMEMBERING through dissociation.

This had to be better than burying it all inside. At least the memories wouldn't be in my body eating away at me. My father's death had brought my trauma over being abandoned to the forefront. After my mother's death, I had unconsciously turned the frame face up - the lack of attachment to her was what was causing my pain. I was certain of it.

*   *   *   *   *   *   *   *

All the layers of trauma were screaming out to me at once. Driving the forty-five minute ride home from my computer class, I roamed the dial of the car radio for something to divert my mind and paused when I heard a familiar voice. The talk show moderator, Steve Edward, was just announcing that the subject that day was "date rape." I had not heard this term before.

Soon tears were flowing down my cheeks, making it difficult to see the road. Women were calling in, describing how they had said 'No', and the man did not listen. All through the years I believed that somehow I had brought it on myself. Perhaps I'd teased him, given him mixed signals. Memories of that awful night became overwhelming, leaving me gasping for breath. All this time, I thought a man had to have put a gun or knife to your head or throat to call it rape.

As I allowed myself to understand that I had indeed been raped, I was flooded with emotions. Anger seemed to take over my whole body. The intensity shocked me. A picture frame could never contain these feelings.

All I could find myself talking to my therapist about was my shame over giving away my daughter. Dr. Middleman got me to see that it would have been impossible to keep my daughter. "You were not married," she explained. "Your means of financial support was to be a stewardess. Who would have taken care of your baby while you traveled? You had no welfare system to help you. You lived in an adult only apartment complex. Where would you have lived?"

I argued back that I would have figured all that out. But, I knew she was right. The way the world was back then, my only alternative would have been to go back home to Pennsylvania with my child, and that would not have worked. Still, I told her that I wondered if I should continue to search for my daughter, since every lead I was able to track down brought up what I had done. I gave my child away!

Dr. Middleman encouraged me to continue my search for my daughter, but to stop looking for my mother, given it appeared I had done all I could. "Write your birth mother a goodbye letter, even if it takes you six months," she suggested. "And tell her exactly how you feel." She felt that hoping was tearing me up emotionally, and that I needed all my energy for the search for my daughter, which was more likely to bring positive results.

How could I possibly write what became to me as THE LETTER? I could never write my mother a goodbye letter. That would mean I was giving up the search. I would never learn about my past. No way could I do something so painful, so final.

By the next week, I had slipped into a deep black hole. The thought of never seeing my mother again overpowered me. Never had I been in such a hole.

From the depths and the darkness of it, I prayed, "Oh God, please help me! I'm scared." Was this what if felt like to be mentally ill? What if I could not climb up the sides of this hole and escape? What if the sides are too slippery? Afraid to be alone, I needed a rope.

In my next therapy session, Dr. Middleman suggested I drop all my various self-help activities, as I was dealing with too many layers at once. She wanted me to concentrate on finding my daughter. Somehow feeling better, I agreed. I believed I had just survived the depths of hell.

* * * * * * * *

Books were such a source of solace and understanding for me. On my next trip to the bookstore, I bought a birth mother's story, *Torn From The Heart*. Deeply moved by how honestly the author expressed her emotions, I wondered if I could transfer my thoughts and emotions to paper as well.

Once I began writing, I could not stop. As the words flowed, so did the tears. My colon went spastic, my face broke out, my eyes burned from staring at the computer screen and my back ached from sitting so long. But painful, long forgotten memories were getting out. Once I wrote through my therapy session, not realizing it until Dr. Middleman phoned. She told me not to worry about missing my session. "Just keep writing. You are doing your own therapy." Memories, instead of coming out in fragments, were now releasing like waves in a storm.

But, as I wrote, I lost interest in finding my daughter. Giving me the number of a local support group called Full Circle, Dr. Middleman suggested I might be afraid that my daughter will reject me. "But," she said. "Time is passing. You might be depriving yourself of knowing grandchildren." But searching was wearing me out and all I wanted to do was numb the pain, shut down, do nothing.

However, the plight of the Holocaust survivors again stirred me. On the fiftieth anniversary of V.E. Day, all the television channels were carrying something on the subject, and I stopped surfing the channels when I came across a ceremony that had been held earlier that day at the Holocaust Museum in Washington, D.C. I had only recently visited there. Again listening to the survivor's stories brought me unspeakable sadness. Listening to their losses was almost too much in my emotional state, but still I watched, mesmerized.

A woman doctor spoke of not being able to celebrate the end of the war fifty years before. She was much too busy taking care of the ill, skeleton-like patients just released from the death camps. "What did we have to celebrate anyway," she asked. "We had lost all our relatives and families." Was this why I related so much to the survivors of the Holocaust? I knew intimately their loss.

"How will you feel meeting your daughter for the first time?" my therapist was asking. My mind went blank and my jaw dropped at the question.

"Throwing up comes to mind," I said. "I would probably be so nervous."

When she challenged me about not having dealt with those emotions, I wondered how anyone could be prepared for such an unknown.

One thing I had promised myself when I went into therapy was to always tell the truth. So, I heard myself admitting, "I hate to say this, but I have never felt anything for my daughter."

Those feelings were locked and sealed away. Whenever I thought about going there, I felt like it was forbidden territory, off limits, a place I had no right to visit. Everyone at the adoption agency had told me I would forget everything, that my daughter had a new life, and I believed them. Besides, I might die opening that locked vault, since I was such a bad person for giving my child away.

But now as I explained everything, I was nearly hysterical. "I feel so guilty not thinking about Bambi every day. Who was I to love? Who was I to think about? I never saw her, never felt her birth. Sometimes it all seems like a dream. If I met my daughter, I am sure she will want me to tell her I thought about her everyday, and that would be a lie."

"You could honestly tell her," Dr. Middleman stated, "that to survive mentally, you had to dissociate yourself from the entire matter, especially having been raped."

As I dried my tears, I brought up the recent Mothers' Day and took in her insights. "You never had a role model concerning motherhood. It is hard for adoptees as they have no mother to tell them what it was like to have you inside them."

My adoptive mother had told my sister and brother about their births, and I had listened. And I had shared such details with my sons. But, perhaps that was the reason I could not connect with my children until after they were born. I needed to know they were real before committing myself to motherhood.

As I thought about pregnancy, anger toward my daughter's birth father (I hated giving him even that title) swelled. I told Dr. Middleman that I could not go there with my daughter, beyond giving her his name and address, which I had found on the Internet, should she ask. Because of him, I was robbed of the joy of my pregnancy with her.

*   *   *   *   *   *   *   *

When I attended the support group meeting of Full Circle, I was happy to find women near my age there. Still, I was the oldest birth mother. Why had I waited so long to come to terms with all that had happened to me as a result of both being adopted and being a birth mother? Of course, I had answered this question many different ways. But I still felt compelled to ask myself and wondered if everyone else was just emotionally healthier.

During the meeting, I discovered that the confidential intermediaries in Michigan were finally trained. Why had I not heard from them? It was six months past the time they were to contact me. They had better be trained!

Before I had a chance to call, I received a response from my request for more non-identifying information. Hoping I was about to learn my daughter's first name, I ripped open the envelope only to find they wanted another thirty dollars. My heart sank. Then I became furious at their power over me.

My friend Ole suggested I just phone the agency and find out what exactly I would be getting for that extra thirty. My first reaction was fear, but then I realized no one there could hurt me any longer.

When I finally finished pacing and was able to call, I learned from the woman I spoke with that, because the agency was a non-profit, they depended on funds for services.

Then the spokesperson dropped a bomb. "For two hundred and fifty dollars, we can do a search for your daughter," she said.

I could not believe what I was hearing. Why wasn't I told about this option months ago?

Suddenly, just connecting with the agency, unleashed a flood of traumatic memories and tears. I had flashbacks of the rape, the relinquishment, the loss, the shame, and the sadness overwhelmed me.

"Are you all right?" the woman asked me.

"Do I sound all right?" I wanted to ask her. No, I wasn't all right. Couldn't they teach social workers more empathy? What did this woman think?

Promising to call back regarding the search when I was more under control, I hung up. In the aftermath, I had a hard time catching my breath. My stomachaches would be following soon. Then more tears came. "God, please make them stop," I prayed.

Two hundred and fifty dollars sounded more like thirty pieces of silver. They were the ones to convince me to relinquish my daughter. They should do the search for free!

*　　*　　*　　*　　*　　*　　*　　*

Hoping to put some distance between myself and that phone call, I decided to run an errand at the mall. But I could not get out of the car once I parked it because I just couldn't stop crying. I knew, if I didn't somehow purge these feelings, I would succumb to despair. Paper! I needed paper to write down my thoughts. After dumping the contents of my purse all over the passenger seat, I could only find scraps. Filling one scrap of paper after another, I pieced together a letter to my daughter.

> Dear Daughter,
>
> When I found out today that for two hundred and fifty dollars I could find you, I became emotionally overwhelmed as all the sadness of letting you go came flooding back. My heart aches, afraid of what I have done (emotionally) to you. It made me realize how different your circumstances were as to why you are on this planet compared to other children who are adopted. You started out your life like me, not normal.
>
> I want to grab Hugh, your birth father, and shake him so hard for what he has done to both of us. Oh, this pain is unbearable. I need someone to hug me and to tell me it will be O.K. I think you would be the only person who could accomplish this task. Yet, why would you want to do that?

My mind's video continues to run. Do I let this agency, who had me surrender you, conduct the search? Dare I take that risk, as they will be in control again? If they cannot find you, then I am back to square one. All I know is, no matter how much it hurts, I need for you to know your roots, something I do not have. While you might not want or need it now, believe me, someday you will.

I hope you are happy and healthy. Hopefully, because of what happened to me, and my being the vehicle to get you to the family you needed, it was the best thing for you. We are all on a journey and yours led you to the family that raised you, just as mine led me to the family that raised me. I only pray it was best for you.

Love, Mom-Sally

My colon went into an uproar again, expressing my feeling of powerlessness in the face of the fact that the agency knew everything and would not tell me without my paying them. Complaining to a friend who was also a birth mother and could really sympathize, she told me she was certain her social worker carried her daughter's file, cabinet and all, on her back during the day and then slept on top of it at night.

What I was realizing through it all was that, when I was in extreme emotional pain, I was able to access my deepest feelings. I was able to write to my daughter, something I could not have done eight months ago. But why did I have to experience all the pain to finally be able to feel all my love for her? Why did it take such pain to enable the love to come out?

* * * * * * * *

My debate about whether to search through the agency or with the confidential intermediary of the state was solved with one phone call. In the early morning hours of June 9, 1995, the Ingham County Probate Court phoned with news that I had been assigned the intermediary whom I had requested, Peg Richer from Grand Rapids, Michigan. They also apologized for forgetting about the three-hour time difference. No apologies were necessary. I was elated.

Right away I called Peg, and found her to be all I had hoped, a warm and understanding person. She represented AIM, Adoption Identity Movement, in Grand Rapids and had been a searcher for eighteen years. My higher power had been working overtime to find such a caring soul. Goodbye agency!

All day long my insides shook as I went about my daily routine, trying to pretend everything was normal. But all I could think about was Bambi. What if the searcher found her dead? But, I knew deep down she was alive. My fantasy was that the search would be quick and she would be found living near the home where she was raised in East Lansing, Michigan. I began to doubt if I was emotionally prepared to meet her, since I could not stop crying when I talked about finding her. I was frightened about what lay ahead. Many birth moms were telling me I had a right to see my child, since I gave her life, but I wasn't sure.

How my sons would handle my finding my daughter was another major concern. Each one had reacted differently when I told them of her existence. Jay brushed it off, responding with his own problem. Kiley suggested I talk with his best friend's mom who was also a birth mother. But it was my youngest son Daniel who gave me the oddest answer.

"Dad must have really loved you to have married you knowing that!" was his comment. I was crushed, but could not say anything. This was not something I had done to myself. Later, Daniel explained in all honesty that he was having a hard time thinking his mom had sex with someone before his dad.

* * * * * * * *

Now that I had a searcher, I tried not to obsess, allowing my higher power to take over as best I could. Whenever I got teary eyed, I knew I just needed to sit down at the computer and write. Then I was able to work through whatever was bothering me, somewhat like releasing the pressure on a valve, a little bit at a time.

Not knowing my birth mother still caused me a great deal of pain. Sometimes the void was unbearable. Nancy Verrier, mother of a biological and an adoptive daughter and psychologist, discovered what she called the Primal Wound. In her book *The Primal Wound* she states:

> What I discovered is what I call the primal wound, a wound which is physical, emotional, psychological, and spiritual, a wound which causes pain so profound as to have been described as cellular by those adoptees who allowed themselves to go that deeply into their pain. I began to understand this wound as having been caused by the separation of the child from his biological mother, the connection to whom seems mystical, mysterious, spiritual and everlasting.

Cellular memories must have been what I was experiencing after seeing the house where I was left. My body had certainly profoundly and mysteriously responded. "Nothing can save the child from that primal pain of separation from the first mother, except keeping them together as mother and child," Verrier wrote, as if reading my mind. This was the conclusion I was coming to.

Further in the book, Verrier tells a story about a woman writing a letter to her birth mom.

> One woman told me that she had intended to write a long letter to her birth mother about whom she had no conscious memory, but for whom she had been thinking about searching. She wanted to explain how she felt about being adopted. She decided to write with her left hand, because she had heard that this would access her right brain and put her more in touch with her feelings. Taking pen in hand she wrote: 'Dear Mommy, come and get me.' After that, she told me, there seemed to be nothing more to say.

Now I understood why I did not want to write that goodbye letter to my birth mother as my therapist had suggested. All I really wanted to write as well was, "Come and get me!"

As I wrote at my computer, thinking deeply about the primal wound, I glanced down at my arm and literally saw a gaping wound, a cut so wide I could look into it. Was this some sort of vision? My arm didn't even have a scratch on it. Was I losing my mind? As I stared at the wound, I saw the ghostly reflection of my mother's face in the pool of blood. Was this literally a cellular memory? Would finding her be like a genie coming out of the bottle of my wound, her face finally able to take shape and become real? Was my wound trying to heal?

I could understand everything Nancy Verrier wrote about.

> It seems as if a mother may be biologically, hormonally and emotionally programmed to bond and respond to her baby at birth in the same way that she was able to do when the fetus was in the womb. That a baby knows its own mother at birth has been proven over and over. What the child has missed is the security and serenity of oneness with the person who gave birth to him, a continuum of bonding from prenatal to postnatal life. This is a profound connection for which the adoptee forever yearns.

> It is my belief, therefore, that the severing of that connection between the adopted child and his birth mother causes a primal or narcissistic wound, which affects the adoptee's sense of self and often manifests in a sense of loss, basic mistrust, anxiety and depression, emotional and/or behavioral problems and difficulties in relationships with significant others. I further believe that the awareness whether conscious or unconscious, that the original separation was the result of the "choice" made by the mother affects the adoptee's self esteem and self worth.

* * * * * * * *

I was exhausted from taking in all this information. From my point of view as an adoptee, I could take in all Nancy Verrier said. But when I thought of my daughter, it was very difficult to think about what the primal wound might have done to her. Like watching a game of ping-pong, my mind kept bouncing back and forth between my birth mother pain and my adoptee pain. Back and forth. Back and forth. I wanted to scream, "Just make it stop!"

I did realize in reading the book that I was fortunate not to be more scarred.

> Adoptees were greatly over represented in psychotherapy. According to 1985 statistics used by Parenting Resources of Santa Ana, California, although adoptees at that time comprised 2-3% of the population of this country, they represented 30-40% of the individuals found in residential treatment centers, juvenile hall and special schools. They demonstrated a high incidence of juvenile delinquency, sexual promiscuity, and running away from home.

The part about running away I could relate to, as I had tried to run away many times growing up. One time, furious and fed up with my mother for blaming me for something I didn't do, I had vowed that this time I would leave. But, as I headed to the front door, my mother beat me to it, covering the door with her whole body. "I will call the police and they will bring you back," she threatened. "You have no money and no place to go."

I knew the political clout my father had with the police and that my venture would be for naught. But now as I looked back I wondered, if I were so intent on running away, why didn't I pack a bag and go out the back door? Instead, for the next few years, I fantasized before falling asleep about saving enough money and finally escaping. However, I never saved a dime.

* * * * * * * *

Even in the face of little hope, I still had to try to find my birth mother. As I faced the hard times I had growing up, I longed for her.

The license plate that Farmer Sundy had scratched into the dirt was from Maryland. If I could get wider coverage in that state, perhaps I could get a lead. For the third time, I contacted the *Baltimore Sun* and again they declined running the story.

The Historical Society of York, replying to a letter I had written months before, suggested I contact the Children's Home in York. I dashed off a letter to them asking if my mother could possibly have gone through their agency. Did they even exist in 1939?

But then the search switched back to my daughter when I received a letter from the court concerning my request for a copy of the papers I signed relinquishing her. My first attempt had come back with a request for a ten-dollar processing fee, which I sent. Now they were returning my check, requiring instead a cashiers check. So far this process had taken six months, and I was still basically at square one. Driven slightly crazy at this point, I sent them the cashier's check they requested and resumed my vigil by the mailbox.

My support group told me, the court normally needed to be petitioned for the relinquishment papers. But, I took it as a good sign that they wanted my money. They weren't saying "No." Those papers should be mine. I signed them, giving away part of my life and I deserved a copy and was determined to get one. No way should I have to petition the court.

Switching searching sides again, I received a letter from the executive director of the Children's Home in York. "Rest assured," the letter read, "If your birth mother was a child at the Children's Home of York and had a baby, the agency would have taken appropriate action if that baby just disappeared, and the baby's identity would have been known." Another lead to nowhere.

Why was I searching anyway? What would it change? All I was doing was shaking everything up in my life that once seemed secure. Now, nothing was stable. This was scary. I needed to get on with my life. But I knew deep down I was not quite ready to stop. As much as I kept being drawn to search for my birth mother, my focus really needed to be on the search for my daughter, because that was the most hopeful.

My searcher, Peg, informed me that my daughter's name did not come up when she did a routine search. That meant she was either married or living elsewhere. Married? Wonderful. Not married but living who knows where? Not wonderful. This meant she would be harder to trace. For some reason I was fixated on believing she was raised in the East Lansing, Michigan area.

While I had Peg on the phone, I asked her if she would give me my daughter's first name. I hated having to use the name Bambi all the time as it sounded so cheap. How could I have ever picked such a name? I realized I couldn't have been in my right mind when that decision was made.

"The courts won't allow me to give it to you. Sorry." Peg said. I really hated having to pay someone for information about my own daughter.

* * * * * * * *

My searching was creating an unsettled feeling among the members of my family, probably because I was changing. Granted, I was in tears most of the time, but it was something else. My support group had told me that every search is also a search for self. This I was finding to be so true. Admitting my hidden secrets was allowing me the freedom to grow emotionally. But one person's growth creates change for everyone, and my family seemed thrown off center by my changing.

No one would admit this was happening. We never discussed the search for my daughter. Nothing was ever mentioned about my having a daughter. My sons did not seem at all interested in the fact they had a sister. All I was met with was silence.

Then there came a shocking phone call from Peg. "After much research," she told me. "I can only gather that your daughter does not live in the United States. She has never had a driver's license issued to her, nor a social security card either."

What she found was that the adoptive father had been collecting social security since the age of sixty-three and in another country.

Remembering the non-identifying information had revealed the adoptive mother had been from Germany, I suggested she search there. Peg had already checked, but that wasn't the case. Since she had never done an international search, Peg offered to refund my money. But, I felt there was something else we could do.

One possibility Peg suggested was to write an open letter to the father in an unsealed envelope and Social Security would forward it to him. This did not feel right to me, as everything I had read advised dealing directly with the adult child. But it was a reassuring option in case all else failed.

Never in all my wildest imaginings could I have believed my daughter lived in a foreign country. I was numb thinking about it. No one I had ever met or talked with ever had to deal with an international search. If only I knew which country. Perhaps, the adoptive mother, being a German Jew had escaped to Holland during the war.

Again, I pressed Peg for my daughter's first name. After discovering she was so far away from me, I needed to know it more than ever. All she would tell me was that my daughter's first name was very unusual, the adoptive mother's maiden name sounded very Jewish, while the adoptive father's last name was quite common. Was it Jones? Smith? Maybe Miller, like my maiden name. The mind rushes to fill in empty places.

I was actually paying a fee for Peg, a total stranger, to have information about my own flesh and blood that I was not entitled to have. My heavens, my daughter was thirty-six years old!

At this point everything felt like it had come to a standstill.

CHAPTER SIX

Again at the point of exhaustion and thinking of calling it quits, I met another angel who wouldn't let me.

Believing Bambi had been raised in East Lansing, I found an adoption site on the Internet, clicked on Michigan and listed my search under East Lansing, hoping someone from there would respond.

Someone did almost immediately. The man, who was to reveal himself to be another angel who, at one time, had lived in East Lansing. His suggestion was, given the population of the town, that my daughter's adoptive father might have been stationed in Germany while in the service, married his German born wife, and moved to East Lansing under the G.I. Bill to go to college.

Thanking him for his insights, I told him I had a chest cold and frankly was worn out from my search. I didn't want to do anything anymore.

His email reply read: "You sound stressed and frustrated with your search at this point. You need to be relaxed, calm and receptive when doing a search. Sure there are dead ends, but isn't that true of every search you do? When you lose your keys and start to look for them, do you always find them in the first place you look? Of course not. They are always in the last place you look. A search for people is that way, too. There are a lot of different places to look, doors to open and passageways to travel. Keep sending official letters and making phone calls. Think of time as working for you instead of against you. Patience and persistence will pay off.

"This is neither a race against the clock nor a repetitive skill game in which you try to better a previous score. It is a hunt. It may take years of alternating cycles of energy, emotion, failure and frustration, followed by withdrawal, regrouping and searching again with a renewed effort. Or it could be over in a matter of days or weeks. That is what makes searching such a challenge. Keep your objective before you at all times, but don't let the search drive you."

He really had my attention. When he asked me to gather all the information I had on my birth parents, I told him I only really had psychic information to follow. But, he insisted I send just facts. Through the facts, he could help me identify clues. What could it hurt to have this stranger help when he is so willing? Perhaps clues were sitting there gathering dust while I kept hitting blank walls. Maybe, just maybe, he would find something none of us were seeing.

He explained he was a dowser, someone with the ability to locate buried objects, foundations, old roads and graves. "My methods," he explained, "have been compared to psychic abilities by others. I maintain a strict reliance on physical indications and on available documentation and research when working with archaeologists, historians, police or cemetery officials. I have worked with psychics and feel some to be surprisingly accurate and others nuttier than fruitcakes. I have a general skepticism of all of them until I see their work."

I had no idea if a dowser could be of help, but I needed guidance. As I looked over the three-page list of evidence I had compiled to send him, I doubted very much that he would find something new. But, even while I was compiling my list, he sent instructions on how to gather more information. With his support and encouragement, I was feeling excited for the first time in months.

Three days later, his stunningly detailed and meticulous email arrived, and I finally learned his name - Richard.

"You have a description of the car and people. You have a point in time, (date, town, time of night) and two locations (or fixes as we navigators call them). That is the time and place of the subsequent placement - where you were found. If, as you say, it was the next lighted place down the road from the first address, then you have, not only a time and place, but also a direction of travel. That could be a very significant clue in your search. It gives you an idea of which direction you came from and hence, possible places to concentrate your search.

"The first house where you were left, the farmer had a hard time determining the color of the car." The farmer had stated it was either blue or black. Therefore, Richard felt, "The time had to have been after sundown and before total darkness. Since it was a rainy night, the time was probably within a half hour of sundown or 5:25 to 5:35 p.m."

He went on. "The population of Thomasville in 1916, was five hundred and forty-three. Most likely, everyone knew each other in this area and the first farmer, seeing the people in the car didn't recognize them. If these strangers were looking for a specific house to leave you, they could have asked the farmer who saw them, but they didn't."

In summing up his impressions, he said, "What do you have at this point? A stocky man and a slender girl/woman are driving in a dark sedan, on a cold and rainy night, with a baby wrapped in worn blankets. They have a mission, to leave the baby at the place where she is certain to be found, and a destination, Thomasville, PA. They probably came from Maryland (as evidence of the license plate and the close proximity of the state), and returned to Maryland that same night, most likely by the same roads they used to enter Thomasville. "I feel you came from either Frederick or Baltimore, Maryland, since they are both about one and a half hours away. With roads leading directly from them to York/Thomasville, both had hospitals. If you were born in a hospital, a record of your birth exists. Since you didn't enter the adoption courts in Maryland, or as a known person, your original birth certificate (if it exists) could not be sealed or kept from you."

Seemingly able to peek back in time as he explained the scenario of events leading up to my abandonment, his comments were similar to what other psychics had said but were far more detailed. He titled them, "Some Deductions and Impressions."

"I feel that the man driving the car was the father of the woman. He was in charge of the situation and was likely an impulsive man, prone to anger and to dominating his family. The sedan was a family type car, not something owned by a teenager in 1939. He was involving the girl in the abandonment of the child, by making her place you on the porch. In so doing, she shared the guilt and could not turn on him or accuse him. After all, it was her fault that this situation existed in the first place.

"During the drive, he assured her that this was the best thing for both her and the child. She was slender, very young and was probably just barely able to travel. You didn't get pneumonia-bronchitis on the porch. You already had it and perhaps had just left a hospital, hence the age of two weeks versus a day or a week.

"The man had not bonded with you and did not care to. The fact that they were driving in poor weather and in the dark indicates that he felt urgency in his mission. Had you been brought home to other family members, his decision most certainly would have been questioned. It made your abandonment easier for him initially.

"The man and girl were not recognized by the Thomasville farmer as being from his town, yet they were determined to leave you there, even though they knew they had been seen by the farmer. If simply getting rid of you was the intent, there are dozens of other towns they could have chosen. This leads me to believe that your natural father was from Thomasville."

Richard went on to say, "The father might have been a member of the Civilian Conservation Corps which moved them around from place to place." He also sensed a "possible military connection, National Guards, the 28th Keystone Division."

All that night I tossed and turned, my mind filled with Richard's searching suggestions and the new information. Finally giving up on sleep, I crawled out of bed at five in the morning. Sipping my black coffee, I wondered if all or even some of what he said was true.

Images of my mother putting me on that porch ran through my mind for the rest of the day.

* * * * * * * *

After doing more research, Richard felt there was no connection to the Senft name in my search. But, to cover all bases, he did a little research in the genealogy section of his daughter's college while waiting for her class to be over. He found a book listing all Maryland men who served in World War II. In it he found one Senft, Harold, born April 1897, who would have been forty-two at the time of my birth. This man still lived in Maryland at that time. At this point, no one could convince me otherwise - Richard was a gift from God.

After reading the long newspaper article about my abandonment, he fine tuned his thoughts about the night's events and gave me more ideas for searching. He wrote, "I always felt the car was a Plymouth and then your news paper article confirms it. You know, it was the car of the year, one of the three leading low priced cars. Chevrolet and Ford being the other two. The price started at six hundred and forty-five dollars for the 'Road King' model.

"I feel the car came from Baltimore, north on Greenmont Avenue/York Road, (old route 111, now called route 45), directly to York and then headed west on Lincoln Highway

(30) to Thomasville. A number of reasons could have gone into the decision to target Thomasville. It may have been planned out in his mind well in advance, but most likely it was an opportune place near York, PA. By leaving you in Pennsylvania, it put the case in the jurisdiction of the Pennsylvania State Police, versus the Maryland State Police. Pennsylvania is where the largest search and publicity would have taken place.

"Check out the *Baltimore Sun* to see if your being found was mentioned. Also, read the York papers carefully. See if any York restaurant owners were quoted as saying that a couple fitting their description stopped for supper. They waited for darkness so they could see that people were home and inside and also so that they could get away without being seen.

"The city of York may have been too well lighted, so they stopped at the first place outside the town. Failing there, they went to the next lighted place and probably continued west on route 30 before doing a u-turn and driving by again on the return trip. Perhaps they would have wanted to check that you had been found. They certainly would not have hung around long, wanting to avoid detection."

His words made me reflect that the psychics I had consulted sensed my mother did not want to give me up, but had no choice. Until now, I believed they were wrong, that they were only telling me what I wanted to hear. But, now Richard was saying the same thing.

"One thing is certain," Richard said. "You were placed on the porch by your mother. The statement of being in good condition when found, and subsequent ill health and intolerance to various formulas, indicates that you were breast fed by the mother."

At this I gasped. My mother breast-fed me! Then she did bond with me. She was forced to give me up because of the times, the strict religious times. It wasn't that she didn't want me. Even though I had always believed this intellectually, it had taken all this time and pain to finally believe it in my heart.

Richard went on to further explain what he thought was the father's behavior. "I have a feeling the couple was Catholic, for no particular reason. Perhaps all the psychics have labeled you Welsh and Irish because of your appearance or mannerisms. The Baltimore Catechism was 'THE' book of Catholic instruction for many years. I do not think the father consulted with a priest or church office prior to his decision to abandon you. If he had, he would have been referred immediately to the Catholic Charities adoption groups. He acted on his own advice. His motives may have been to keep his daughter's and family's reputation and future from being 'stained;' or, economics, to keep from having to raise another child. Possibly both."

Perhaps that is why I had reacted so strongly and with such anger to the article in the CUB newsletter that "the majority of children placed for adoption today come from poor 'Bible Belt' areas where many of the poorest families live and where religious belief often rules out abortion as an option." I had been wrapped in an old blanket, most likely by a poor mother who could not stand up to the stigma imposed on her.

In closing, Richard suggested that I was not a foundling in the state of Maryland, only in Pennsylvania, and I could and should request a search of all live birth records for a white (Caucasian) female, born in January, 1939 to a single mother between the ages of 16-19. Probably listed as her first child (no siblings).

* * * * * * * *

Stumbling over the suitcase I was hurriedly packing for my trip to the annual adoption convention in New York, I grabbed the ringing phone. Peg was on the other end. "I have news about your daughter," she said.

Everything slowed down, as I slid onto the edge of the bed.

"I promised you I would call before you left for your trip," I heard her say. "After receiving Bambi's file from the adoption agency, I did a little investigative work and found that the adoptive family moved to Holland at least thirty years ago."

Somehow I had known it was Holland. This was why Bambi didn't have a social security number.

"The adoptive mother's father was Jewish, but the family is now Lutheran," Peg went on.

My daughter was mirroring my life. I was Lutheran, and now I'm Jewish. She was Jewish and now Lutheran. Bizarre.

As it sunk in that my little girl did not grow up in the United States, it felt like I had been kicked in the stomach. I had not given my child to a foreign family. My daughter was an American. Perhaps it was because I had been raised in a city that was steeped in history, but I felt an enormous loss that my daughter would never experience the thrilling patriotic feelings when seeing the American flag billowing in the breeze.

As a little girl, I learned all the songs and marched along with the Reserved Officers Training Corps from Dickinson College every Tuesday and Thursday when they marched past our building. When I heard them singing, "Over hill, over dale, as we hit the dusty trail, and the caissons go rolling along," I would drop everything and run outside. I knew they would probably have to fight in a war, and I was proud of them. I sang their songs in a loud, ringing voice.

Bambi would never feel the pride of singing the national anthem at sporting events. In high school, as a majorette, I would stand at attention when the flag was raised and the band played the national anthem. What did my daughter celebrate? The queen?

I found my husband, Ross, working on a project in the garage. When I told him how upset I was, he said, "Holland is a great place to be raised and, knowing you, you would probably be satisfied knowing that she was raised in a loving home and was happy."

But, I was not so sure. Of course I wanted that, but I wanted more. I wanted her back, as dumb an idea as that was. I could never hope to get her back. At least now, I knew in which country to search.

* * * * * * * *

The three by five cards full of searching suggestions from Richard were stuffed into my carry-on for the convention. Any search material for my daughter was left behind. The search for her would have to wait for now.

As if waiting there for me, the intense pain I experienced at the last year's convention unexpectedly came rushing back, overwhelming me. In no way was I prepared for the intense feelings that were overtaking my body. After taking a plane, bus, train and cab to get to the convention, I wasn't even certain I could go to the first event. So, I decided to skip the plenary session and fortified myself instead with a hearty breakfast.

Strengthened, I headed off to the first workshop - "The Birth Mother Filter: How the Birth Parent Experience Can Effect Current Daily Living, A look at Feelings, Communication, and Coping Skills." My own coping skills in the workshop appeared to be to put up as much armor as I could in order not to feel anything. I sat in the chair feeling like a porcupine, my needles protecting me from any emotional pain that might head my way. Taking in very little about what was being said, I startled myself, and the speaker by firmly stating, "No" when the suggestion was made to try to forgive the birth father. My protective shield grew stronger.

The morning sessions over, I sat with friends having lunch at an outdoor cafe, dwarfed by the tall buildings of Manhattan. The subject for discussion around our table was anger. Distracted and exhausted, I watched the people rushing by on their lunch break. When asked if I was angry, I managed to respond that I didn't have anger issues. I just felt sad. But my friends all reminded me of how angry I had been at the agency for charging me two hundred and fifty dollars to do a search. Of course, feeling anger is normal. My realization helped me feel a little bit better.

Reubon Pannor, psychologist, social worker and author of *The Adoption Triangle*, a classic in adoption literature, was speaking next. His statement concerning bonding was one I found very interesting:

> One of the important myths to be debunked today is the myth of bonding. This excuse is being used today by attorneys trying to prevent birth parents from reclaiming their adopted children. If the return of children placed without benefit of fully legal relinquishments and adoption decrees is delayed, these lawyers reason that bonding with the adoptive parents has taken place and that it would not be in the best interest of the child to remove it from the adoptive home. Since the myth of bonding is so widely believed in our culture, this defensive strategy can work well in the legal arena."

He also said:

> Bonding is something that can only be understood to occur between the gestational mother and the infant. It begins in utero and continues after birth. Any other type of link is an attachment, not a bond. Only a mother can bond with her child and adoptees attach to their adoptive parents.

I had to hear his opinion in person, and so I stood up in the audience and asked if the difference between bonding and attachment really made a difference. "Surely I must have bonded with my child, but did I? I felt very bonded with my adoptive dad, but are you saying I was only attached to him?"

Pannor responded that bonding was actually physiological. Confused, but not knowing what else to ask, I sat down.

Since I hadn't nursed Bambi, did we bond in utero? If Richard was right about my mother breast feeding me, did I have a stronger bond with my mother than my daughter would have with me? I still didn't get it. Does bonding mean, at least to those in the adoption triangle, BOND - Bring Original Nurturer on the Double? Maybe?

*　　*　　*　　*　　*　　*　　*　　*

That night I fell into bed exhausted, hoping to escape the emotional pain of the day with sleep. But sleep did not come. My tears still seemed unexplainable. All I could hope for was to feel better in the morning. Instead, I felt worse.

For the first session the next day, a therapy group took the place of a canceled session entitled Codependence in Relationship to Adoption. Our large group formed a circle with our chairs and we all began to introduce ourselves and tell the others what part of the triad we represented and anything else we felt we wanted to add. When it came my turn, I found I could not talk without crying.

Just when I was wishing I could figure out how to escape the room, I was approached by another angel. This lovely lady introduced herself as a social worker and an adoptee who had been raised in Holland! On top of that, she now lived in Michigan very near Peg, my searcher. She offered to help with my search, since she spoke the same language as in Holland. Fate had to have brought her to me. Unseen hands must guide our searches, wanting our reunions to happen as much as we all do, I thought to myself.

After taking a long walk and having quiet time alone to reflect, I decided that I needed to take care of myself and only attend a few sessions a day. In dire need of support, I headed back to the convention to attend a support group gathering. Remembering the intense pain and primal crying that had resulted last year after exposing the secret of having given up my daughter, I hesitated before going in. But, knowing important emotional work happened during these sessions, I entered the room. The only seats left were in the back, outside of the circle. But, this was perfect for me. Having a little distance from the group enabled me to listen to the others tell of their painful stories, and quietly reflect on my own. I could almost convince myself I was a bystander.

One woman's sobs at not being allowed to meet her newly found birth mother brought to mind the crying out of a trapped, hurt animal. How could a mother not want to meet her own child? From the corner of my eye, I watched a recently reunited daughter grab her birth mother's hand and hold on for dear life, their body language speaking volumes: "I am so lucky to have found you, and I will never let you go ever again."

As I glanced around the room, I noticed a psychiatrist and author of *Second Choice: Growing Up Adopted*, his memoir of being adopted, wiping tears from his eyes. Does this pain continue forever, even after finding loved ones, becoming a psychiatrist to overcome it or activist to face and fix it?

Leaving the room, I felt the image of the weeping psychiatrist and the clinging mother and daughter etched deep within in my soul. My emotions were completely spent, and I would not be attending any more of the convention. The remainder of my time back east would be spent searching for my birth mother.

* * * * * * * *

First, I just had to meet Reverend and Mrs. Senft and see for myself if this woman did indeed look like me. My brother and sister-in-law along for company, I watched the young man bouncing a ball in front as we pulled up to the Senft home. To my disappointment, he informed me that the Senfts had moved six years before to the Lutheran Retirement Village in Chambersburg. Visiting them there was not possible.

Instead, I stopped into the Cumberland County Historical Society, located in my hometown, and which seemed to have been around as long as I could remember, although it used to be next to the Strand Theater, which was now no longer there. As a young girl, standing in line for tickets in front of the Strand, I observed that it only seemed like old people went into the Historical Society. And now I was walking in.

While I made myself comfortable in front of the microfilm machine, the man next to me leaned over and asked what name I was searching. "My own," I softly responded, and told him the quick version of my abandonment.

His was a similar story, though he was an orphan, not a foundling and not adopted. He had been placed in the Hershey School for Boys, which is where he grew up. He was looking for his grandfather's name - Sundy!

Before getting back to his search, he gave me the name and phone number for the head of the Genealogical Society of which he was a member. Wishing me luck, he warned me not to get side tracked by all the other interesting information I would find in there. Scanning the room, I wondered how many others were searching for their own identities, too.

It wasn't long before I ran across the same article I had discovered in the little drawer of my mother's desk when I was a young girl. Again, I was overwhelmed by emotions I thought I had under control.

In the article, originally published in the Hanover, Pennsylvania paper, dated February 8, it was stated that I had been abandoned on Monday, February 6, not the 5th as reported in other sources that had written of my abandonment as a rainy evening of Sunday, February 5. Remembering Richard's suggestion, I looked up the weather report for those two days and discovered it had rained on February 6th only. This must have been the true date I was found then. Looking back, I realized I had already had a clue from Janet Senft that the true date was actually the sixth. When I had mentioned being found on a Sunday evening, she had responded puzzled that she was surprised to know that as her family was always at church on Sunday evenings. At the time, I dismissed her confusion thinking it was possible her mother may have been sick or something else had happened that Sunday evening to prevent them from going.

Adding that extra day was enough to place it into the realm of possibility that I was an Aquarian, not a Capricorn, which felt right to me. Somehow just knowing this was settling to me. In a funny way, it made me feel rather normal!

Forgetting the man's warning about not getting distracted reading articles while searching, I went off on a tangent and began having fun. Reading the newspapers from January and February of the time I was born, I learned the Civil Liberties Bureau was being set up as a division of the Justice Department in Washington, D.C. Beef sirloin steak was advertised for 27 cents per pound, and the Kentucky thaw caused 7,000 families to flee their homes when melting snow and rain sent the Ohio and Tennessee rivers over their banks.

There was a world's fair in New York City, and the Oscar winning movie of the year was *Gone With The Wind.* The top tunes were "The Beer Barrel Polka," "Over the Rainbow" and "God Bless America." The Yankees won the World Series and Joe Louis was the heavy weight boxing champ. The average yearly income was $1,729, and the life expectancy was 59.7 years. And of course there was lots of news about the war.

Somehow, I was able to connect with my past as I poured over all this information. Not having a personal history had me craving one. But, now as I left the historical society, I gained important information about myself. I learned the real day I was found, felt certain of my horoscope sign and got a better sense of what the world was like back then.

That evening, I phone Mr. Robert Viquers Jr., head of the Capital Area Genealogical Society, the man Bill Sundy had referred me to that day.

"You were most likely born at home," he said, "as my wife comes from the same area and all ten children, up until 1944, were born at home. You may or may not have a birth certificate." He suggested I check the State Police files.

* * * * * * * *

Armed with quarters for the copy machine, my writing pad, notes from Richard and directions to the State Archive building in Harrisburg, I climbed into my rental car feeling like a racehorse at the starting gate. "Now," I prayed, "please let me find the State Police report of my abandonment taken by Corporal Snyder and Private Sneeder."

Before being allowed admittance into the record room, I was given a form to fill out. They wanted my name, address and what subject I wanted to search. What was I to say? That I was looking for my Mom and Dad in the police records? I left that part blank.

I was then instructed to put all my search material, purse, everything away in a locker and pay a dollar for the lock. The only thing I was allowed to keep was my pencil and paper. Without Richard's notes as a guide, I could only hope I could remember everything he had told me to investigate.

Entering the room, I was given further instructions to ask the man at the far desk for what I needed. Standing before the desk, I asked for the State Police Records and received a thin file folder. Subjects were listed in alphabetical order and stored elsewhere.

I could have asked for the file of the Klu Klux Klan, which the police investigated from 1923 through 1950. Included would be the Klan's mailing list for Pennsylvania and New Jersey, their enlistment papers by county and their publications. It was comforting to know the police were doing their job.

There were records of special duty by the State Police protecting Franklin Delano Roosevelt, 1936-1945; Wendall Wilkie, 1945; Thomas Dewey, 1944-48; General Douglas MacArthur, 1951; Dwight D. Eisenhower, 1952-55; and Richard Nixon, 1952-1960. But I was becoming sidetracked again.

Getting back to my search, I ran across an article dated February 20, 1939, carrying the names of Arthur Snyder, Troupe B, who was eligible for promotion to sergeant in the crime division, and another on William Sneeder.

Since I was not allowed to bring my search notes with me, I was not sure if these were the policemen's names I was to investigate. Hoping I was remembering correctly, I filled out the forms requesting their files, along with three other subjects of possible further exploration. Feeling time slipping away as I waited in line to hand my requests to the commander at the desk, I wanted to yell, “Get those boxes in here now!” Assigned to seat number three to wait for the material, I began to feel like only a number.

The metal cart, its wheels clacking across the floor, finally arrived with the boxes of files I ordered. Then someone in authority yelled out, “You can only bring out one file from a box at a time!” All the rules were making me a little irritated. Blowing the dust off the top of one box, I returned to my assigned number three seat, ready to comply.

While the material was interesting, I found no criminal police reports. Mostly there were financial and personnel records. Ordering four more boxes yielded no better results.

Certain I was going to find something to help my search along, I felt terribly let down. When I learned in 1984, that the records had been purged, I should have believed them instead of wasting my time.

To console myself, I stopped at the State Museum’s gift shop and purchased a handmade Liberty Bell cookie cutter.

* * * * * * * *

Next stop was York Hospital for the hospital records. As I pulled into the parking lot, I was met with a rush of surprisingly intense emotions. How could this place elicit such powerful feelings when I was only a week or so old when admitted there? As I stared through the front windshield at the entrance to the hospital, I tried to imagine Mr. Senft walking through them with me in his arms.

Maneuvering around the construction happening in the parking lot was a diversion from my feelings, but as I stood at the door, I found myself hesitating, afraid to go in. Finally my need to know overrode any fears. Asking for directions, I then went directly to medical records, certain I would find something new. This seemed my last hope.

When I asked at the reception desk for my records from 1939, I was met with a puzzled look. The lady excused herself to go consult with her supervisor. Before the phone at the desk even rang, I knew somehow it was for me. Nervously, I coiled the cord around my hand as I spoke with the supervisor. Everything seemed to stop as I heard her say that all records prior to 1962 had been destroyed. A black gloom settled over me. "You mean nothing is left of my time here? Nothing?" Suddenly I felt like I didn't really exist.

Hearing the dismay in my voice, the supervisor said that records were never kept back then as they are now, so there probably wasn't much information in them anyway. She seemed to be offering an excuse.

I explained a little curtly that being in their hospital for six weeks should entitle me to some records. I needed them for medical reasons. Reluctantly, she agreed to look in the archives just to be certain.

Taking a seat in one of the chairs lining the narrow hallway, I stared at the word "Archive," printed on the glass door directly in front of me. The supervisor crossed in front of me and entered the room. As the door closed quickly behind her, I could only pray that she would find some information.

A few minutes later, the phone rang. It was the supervisor for me again. All the information they had was written on a 3 x 5 card: 'Baby X, admitted February 6, 1939.' My God. This place, where I lay for six weeks, had played such a huge role in my life and I had been reduced to a 3 x 5 index card. If only she could have had the decency to give me this information personally. This had been my last hope. Now the search for my parents was over.

Tears streaming down my face, I walked slowly down the hall, my feet dragging almost as if the floor itself were holding me back from leaving for some reason. As I searched for an excuse to linger, I spotted a bulletin board and walked over to take a closer look.

On it was a clipping from the Sunday York paper dated September 17, 1995, telling of a book that marked the hundredth anniversary of the York Hospital Auxiliary. Was this why I felt a need to stay, to find out about this book?

A lovely older woman, a volunteer with more time to spare, contacted the public relations office of the hospital who, in turn, directed me to the library where the book, called *That Sovereign Knowledge*, was kept. With great anticipation, I began reading. Anything with 1939 caught my eye. Carefully turning the pages, I came upon a picture of the nursery with all its bassinets lined up in a row. Excited at my discovery, I wanted to run around and show everyone and anyone that one of these bassinets had been my home for six weeks. Instead, I kept silent. Who would understand what I was feeling anyway?

In the quiet of the library, I stared out the window observing the autumn colored leaves on the trees. My soul felt like it was dripping tears. This was no time to reflect, however, and I went back to my reading. One article spoke about how an iron lung, which had been at the hospital on a trial basis, had saved a baby's life. Since polio was making steady inroads into the country, the board decided to purchase it. Reading this brought back memories of the fear of getting polio. I had not been allowed to attend the Carlisle Fair for fear of getting the horrible crippling disease in crowds.

Then I turned the page to a picture of a Dr. Smyser, head of Pediatrics from 1915 to 1945. My heart fluttered, as I knew with everything in my being that this was the doctor that had taken care of me so many years before.

Nurse Ness wrote that, "Dr. Smyser was a gentle person, lover of wild flowers, a fine doctor and a personable human being."

Another nurse said that, "He would come day or night for anything and had few patients that died."

This man had kept me alive. I was sure of it. I made a photo static copy. I was so certain.

Though finished with the book now, I still did not want to leave the hospital and looking around the beautiful library, I wondered what else I could research. After telling the head librarian what my mission was, she suggested I look in the archive room.

Boxes were stacked one on top of the other, making it impossible to know where to start. Then, my eye caught a label titled 'School of Nursing' on a large box, and I decided to start there.

In it, I discovered minutes of a meeting of the York School of Nursing dated February 6, 1939, the very day I was admitted. The minutes told of a senior student who had been suspended from school for three weeks for keeping company with a married man. If she did not promise to break up with him, she was going to be dismissed from school.

Another note in the minutes told of a nurse who had returned to the hospital intoxicated and was suspended for one year. Apparently all the nursing students had to attend a prayer service each morning.

Reading the minutes helped me realize just how puritanical society was back then. In such a strict culture, no woman pregnant out of wedlock could hope to keep her child.

With nothing left to read or research, I could no longer postpone leaving the building. My whole being, for some reason, seemed extremely sad to be leaving this comfortable place.

CHAPTER SEVEN

Since I was in York, I decided to make one last search for information at the Historical Society. As soon as I could stop the tape from flying off the microfilm machine, I settled down to work. Out of the blue appeared the photo of myself as an infant, Nurse Alfretta Glassford holding me in her arms. This was the first time I knew which paper had carried the story. It was the February 9, 1939 issue of the York Dispatch. I made a copy.

As my friend Richard had suspected, there was a Civilian Conservation Corps camp in nearby Clearfield. Perhaps one of the men at the camp was my birth father. I wrote down all that information.

Then, because Janet Senft had mentioned she went to a Reformed church, one that shared space with a Lutheran Church, I wrote down information about Wolf's church that fit that description. Perhaps it was a clue. The psychic in New York had felt there was a religious connection to my abandonment. Perhaps someone's son from this church got a girl pregnant and then put her on the Senft's porch because they knew them from church. Who knew?

Suddenly, the long newspaper article about me popped up, the one that used to hang for years over the Senft family radio. For the first time I noticed that it was the local police sub station that handled the investigation. I made a copy.

Next, I looked in the Polk City Directory for York County for the address of the C.E. Stevens Paper Bag Company. Since it was in one of their bags that I was found, perhaps there would be a clue. But, I found no listing.

A volunteer got me an old atlas showing what the area looked like in 1939. When I told her I was looking for Thomasville and for two churches in Paradise, we discovered a Catholic orphanage there. Paradise became known for this orphanage. The town was right next to Thomasville. The volunteer said there was also a Catholic Church there called St. Mary's.

My heart stopped for a second when I learned of the orphanage, and an electric charge ran through my body. After hearing stories from searchers of hair standing on end, goose bumps and the like when the correct clues and names were discovered, I knew to pay attention to my body's wisdom.

After packing up my carryall, I asked for directions to Thomasville so that I could check to see if they had a post office, and if the residents had to pick up their mail there in 1939, or was it delivered. Was it mandatory for residents to have their name on the post mailbox? If so, then the man and woman who dropped me off would have known the name of the people living at the home. But the post office was closed.

Perhaps if I drove down the highway my mother had to have driven that night, something might trigger inside me. As I drove toward the Senft house, I noticed many more houses than I had remembered from my last trip.

Instead of clarity, I got confusion. My parents could have dropped me on any one of these porches. Why did they pick the one they did?

Discouraged, I decided not to visit the two churches in Paradise. What for? Nor would I pay a visit to the Rev. Senft and his wife. I just didn't care anymore.

* * * * * * * *

Loaded down with all my search material, I kicked the car door shut with my foot, marched into my brother's house and announced once again, "I quit! At least when I play the slots in Las Vegas, I get a few coins back for my effort, something to entice me to play more. After all these weeks of searching, I have not received even one token. That's it! I'm done! I've had it! Finished! The end!"

Exhausted, I called my girlfriend Donna and she said, "You know, wanting to quit tells you something, too."

Then, later that night, an amazing thing happened. Around ten o'clock, my cousin's wife, Lynn, phoned. She was out of breath from rushing home to tell me the news. Her women's club had a psychic as a guest speaker at their meeting that night. At one point, the psychic had asked if anyone had any questions. When no one raised their hand, Lynn raised hers and said her husband's cousin was looking for her natural parents. Could she help? The psychic had seen that my parents were from the King of Prussia area outside of Philadelphia. She thought my mother was Italian.

Although she said she didn't know much about psychics, Lynn felt this one was good. She had been on the Maury Povich Show.

Only two hours before I had decided to end my search. Was this an answer from above? I decided to have a personal reading. I had nothing else planned.

* * * * * * * *

The next morning, I found myself feeling uneasy about making the call. Do psychics really know things? Why was I hesitating? Finally getting up my nerve, I phoned. She was with a client. Could I call back at noon?

When we had a chance to talk, she told me she was going out of town. So a reading in person was out of the question. But she could give me a reading over the phone at three that afternoon. I said, Fine."

Still nervous about having the reading, I wore myself out killing time. At three o'clock, I found myself in a fast food restaurant, still trying to decide. Dashing back to my brother's I reluctantly dialed the psychic's number.

At first she had me just talking about anything. Hearing my voice would trigger things for her. So, I talked about what the beauty of the autumn and the fall leaves meant to me, pausing once in a while to see if I had said enough. The whole thing felt foolish.

All of a sudden, the psychic began talking, telling me things about myself. Some things I agreed with, some things I didn't. I wrote cryptic notes to help me remember everything later.

Then she said, "Your birthday is February 6, 1939." I told her no, that was the day I was found. In that case, she felt my real birthday was January 27. At this point, I was not getting excited about anything. Other psychics had said, January 18, January 23, and now January 27. At least she was in the ballpark, and confirmed I was an Aquarian.

"You are a teacher reincarnate. You came into the first cycle and into the next cycle as that." I had no idea what she was talking about. Then, she started speaking rapidly. "Your father was older in age than your mother. Very Irish. Your mother was Italian."

When I protested being Italian since I was so fair complected, she said that people from the northern part of Italy are fair skinned. "Your mother had fair skin," she said. "Your father was a teacher, your mother a student. Both had a strong Catholic faith. Your mother was among friends, so her family was not aware of your birth. As I told your friend last evening, I see your roots coming from the Philadelphia area, King of Prussia. Your mother was in school and did not return home, so no one would know of your birth. The area where you were left had been visited, as relatives of your father lived there."

"Your father was a teacher/professor at an all girls Catholic school. Investigate anyone associated with such a school. He was a very learned person, had a fast temper, witty, fiery (Irish blood), says what he means, is very direct. Your mother was in awe of his wisdom. She was sensitive, laid back, and dominated by the father."

I told her I married a brilliant man, much like the description of my father. Older, too. She said, "History repeats itself, you know."

Deep down, I felt this information was correct. It had to be. The hairs on my arms were standing at attention.

She continued. "You have a language you can relate to, but can't speak." I knew she meant Italian. Ross and I went to Italy on our honeymoon.

Then she shocked me. "Your mother has seen you growing up. In fact, she has spoken to you, but you weren't aware of it. She has observed you." The psychic in New York had said the same thing, and that my mother had lived nearby.

"Your father had a ruddy, fair complexion, reddish brown hair, precise nose - unusual and large. He had a dimple on his chin. Mother had medium to light hair, a Mary Tyler Moore type mouth, thick brows, five feet, six inches tall, thinly built, curly hair."

My brain was screaming. This was so similar to the description the New York psychic had given me of my mother. From this description, I take after my father as I have red highlights in my hair, a dimple in my cheek and at the end of my nose, and I am of stocky build like him. From my mother I got my sensitivity and the shape of my mouth.

Feeling overwhelmed, I said, "I am so confused with all this information. Maybe it means I should quit searching. This is just too hard!" Firmly, yet quietly, she responded, "You have been given the information. Ask from within."

Just before hanging up, I told her of the search for my daughter who lived in Holland. The psychic said she suddenly had goose bumps all over. "My husband is from Holland," she said. "The educational system there is wonderful." Nothing came to her about my search for my daughter. But we realized we were both born in the same month of the same year, and both allergic to animal by-products. We had made a real connection.

For a long time, I sat frozen in my chair. Where could I have met my natural mother? Who could it have been? Trying to conjure all the people I had met in my life, I could think of no one that fit that description.

With my energy high from the psychic reading, I left the house for the library to research the C. E. Stevens Paper Company. The search took two hours. After all these years, I found they were still in business. My last remaining clue was still there, headquartered in Baltimore.

Now that I was on a roll, I looked up IBM in Holland, believing that was the company my daughter's adoptive father worked for. Found it! They were located in Amsterdam. In case Peg needed the information, I copied it all to send to her for my daughter's file.

That evening, on the way to get something to eat, I told my sister-in-law what the psychic had said. Emily, who did therapeutic touch, often incorporating it into her nursing skills, exclaimed she would love to try therapeutic touch on me right that moment. "Wow!" she said. "You are full of energy. Can't you feel the energy as I move my hand over your arm?" Too busy trying to assimilate all I had learned that day, I couldn't feel anything.

* * * * * * * *

As I lay in bed the next morning, I was still attempting to pull all the information together from the various psychics. Some of it was the same and some of it different. One thought the man in the car was my father, another that my birth father was an older man, perhaps a teacher. One confirmed Richard's feeling that the man has a temper. They all seemed to see something about religion. Several thought my mother had watched over me. How could I make sense out of any of it without proof? I wondered what a psychic would say about me to my daughter if she sought such information.

My brain worn out from thinking about it all, I climbed out of bed and got dressed. As I leaned over to lace up my ankle high boots, a light filled my head as if a light bulb had just been switched on in my brain. A picture began to emerge.

As vivid as anything, I saw a man driving a dark sedan. A woman was sitting on the passenger side holding a baby. All I saw was their outer clothing. The woman's coat did not completely cover her dress, so the bottom half showed. The fabric seemed to have a flower design. The baby was wrapped tightly, cocoon-like, in a blanket.

At first out of focus, the image of the man became clear. He was wearing a black suit with white at the collar. "Oh, my God!" I thought, completely forgetting about lacing up my remaining boot. Truth overtook me as I grabbed for the bedpost. My father was my mother's priest! Blinking lights went off in my brain, like ones along the Las Vegas strip: "Your father was a priest!"

Sitting on the edge of the bed, I thought this felt right. All the pieces of the puzzle now fit. No wonder they dumped me on the porch! They never could have taken me to an adoption agency. Having this information gave me such peace. It was impossible to explain my certainty, but I knew without a doubt that what I "saw" was true. Ask within the psychic had told me yesterday.

All the next day I was haunted by the realization that I had been born Catholic. With only a few days left and with a need to immerse myself in the mundane, I drove to the apple orchards to bring back fresh Pennsylvania apples to my friend in California. After purchasing the apples, I proceeded on my way until I saw a large yard sale and squealed my rental car to a stop.

Tables were piled high with antiques and collectibles. A large tin of buttons caught my eye. Collecting them was a hobby, and I eagerly searched through the tin for buttons I did not have. As I searched, I came across two objects that weren't buttons. One was a Lutheran pin, my daughter's religion and the one I grew up with, and the other was a Saint Francis medal, from my ancestral religion maybe.

As I sorted the buttons I wanted to take, I also wanted to see if there were any other objects in the tin. There were none but the two pins. Of course, I bought them both. They seemed to have been waiting for me to claim them, a validation and a symbol of my recent discoveries.

On my last day before going back home, I went to the library to look up the King of Prussia area of Philadelphia. On the way into the library, I had to negotiate around the annual Carlisle Crafts Fair. A woman with her arm loaded with craft items, told me that the King of Prussia area, which was near Valley Forge, was known for a huge shopping mall there.

As a child, on the way to downtown Philadelphia to shop at the large John Wannamaker department store, we would pass through Valley Forge. Whenever we passed through, my mother always told the story of how so many soldiers, under the leadership of George Washington, froze to death during the bitter winter from lack of supplies. Finally fortified, the Continental Army was able to carry on the fight for five more years. The idea of freezing to death was haunting.

While there, I decided to investigate the university and college encyclopedias for Catholic all girl schools. Scanning down the list, one actually stopped my heart from beating for a second. The College of Notre Dame of

Maryland, founded in 1873, was located in Baltimore. By now, I knew to trust when a name jumps out and causes a reaction. Perhaps this was where I should look.

*　　*　　*　　*　　*　　*　　*　　*

As I boarded the plane back to California, the cold wind whipped through my clothes like a signature kiss from a long time ago. While waiting for the plane to depart, my mind flashed back over all I had experienced on this trip. All the new information had changed my life. I couldn't wait to return home and begin investigating whether or not my father was a priest.

Back home I discovered, while checking my emails, that Richard had continued working on my case while I was gone, and had more information. He felt he possibly might have located the detective who would have investigated my abandonment case. The number he had could be someone the detective was related to, since it wasn't certain the detective was still alive. As it turned out, when I called, the couple who answered had no idea who I was talking about.

A few days later, a package from Richard arrived. The package contained pictures of 1939 Plymouths, ones that would be similar to the description of the dark sedan I was in the night of my abandonment and, just in case, a picture of a new Oldsmobile from that year. Also included in the package was a list of colleges from the Encyclopedia Britannica, a Maryland manual listing state institutions that received state money, and a copy of a page from a Baltimore phone book, listing all the Senfts in that area.

The cars looked like the sort gangsters would drive. In his note, Richard explained he had included the Oldsmobile so I could see the difference in the placement of the headlights. He noted, "The Oldsmobile had its headlights between the fenders and the hood. All General Motors and Ford cars had this arrangement in 1939. The Plymouth's headlights were in the fenders for the first time that year. This may have allowed the farmer to identify the car as a Plymouth. Even in dim light, if it was a 1939 model, the headlights would have been wider apart than almost any other car on the road." If he hadn't pointed it out, I honestly would have never seen the difference.

* * * * * * * *

Now that I was feeling less jet lagged, I wanted to follow through on my last lead and contact the C.E. Stevens' Company, maker of the paper bag. In my letter to them, I explained that I had been found in one of their paper bags and wished to know their distribution base in 1939.

Just as I finished the letter, my intermediary, Peg, phoned. She wanted me to know their contact in Michigan had faxed her relative in Amsterdam for help in locating my daughter. This request produced the adoptive parent's name, address and phone number. The next step was to check marriage certificates in the area in hopes of getting Bambi's new name and address.

Peg had also found out that people in Holland were not in the habit of telling their adopted children that they were adopted, which suddenly made me feel very insecure about what I was doing. Was this the best thing for my daughter? Even though I was desperately searching for my mother, would I be hurting my daughter by finding her?

A few days later, in the early evening, I received a call from the receptionist at the C. E. Stevens Company to let me know that the CEO of the company would be out of town for the next three weeks. "I was very touched by your letter," she said. "I know what you are going through, because I found my birth father last year. I also know how important receiving information is when searching and didn't want you to think you had been forgotten. I will have our CEO call you as soon as he returns."

This woman's call amazed me for two reasons. First, I had not included my phone number in the letter, so that she had to have made an effort to reach me. Second, I was shocked to learn the company had moved from Baltimore years ago. They were now located in Hagerstown, Maryland, not far from the Maryland/Pennsylvania border. How had my letter ever even reached them? And, on top of everything, the company no longer made paper bags. They now made containers for Italian food. Italian!

Stopping by the local library, I learned the process of requesting a list of the all girl Catholic colleges in Maryland and Pennsylvania was going to take a while. The librarian thought she might be able to get such a list from the University of California, Los Angeles. Just having something in process felt good, so I didn't mind the wait.

Driving back up the hill to home, I noticed a garage sale nearby. Figuring that this late it must be closed, I decided to stop anyway, just in case. I arrived as they were boxing up remaining items for charity. When I spotted a large box filled with books, I suggested they donate them to the used bookstore at the library. Exhausted after a long day of selling, they just looked at me and said, "For a dollar, you can take them all."

At home, sorting the books into bags I could easily carry into the library, setting aside the ones I might want, I ran across an old dictionary. At first I thought this was one I didn't need and tossed it into the library bag. But then I remembered that other things besides words were often listed in dictionaries.

So, I retrieved the book and opened to the first page. It was published in 1937. Flipping to the table of contents, my heart skipped a beat. Listed were colleges and universities in the United States and Canada. Quickly, I flipped to page 1,264. Not only did they list the colleges, they also denoted whether coed, women, men, and the year the college was founded.

Angels were watching over me.

CHAPTER EIGHT

A few days later, awakening on the morning of my daughter's thirty-fifth birthday, I could feel that all my exhilaration was gone. She was celebrating somewhere in Holland, and I felt terribly sad not knowing how she was going to celebrate this day we both shared.

Then the phone rang, interrupting my thoughts. It was Peg. She wanted me to know that her contact in Amsterdam was unable to find a marriage certificate for my daughter, which meant my daughter wasn't married.

"They did find one more name listed under the adoptive parents' name in the phone book." Peg said. "But, after checking it out, they discovered it was listed by a female born in 1961 with different first and middle names from your daughter's. At this point we have no idea where your daughter is."

My suggestion to call the adoptive father, posing as an old friend, to get her number fell on deaf ears. I was so tired of knocking my head against brick walls. All I wanted was to meet my daughter.

* * * * * * * *

Thirty-five years after my daughter's birth, I finally discovered why I could not remember her birth date. In her book *Shadow Train*, Patricia Taylor, a registered nurse, family and child therapist, birth mother and mother to four children she raised, explained that the reason many birth mothers could not remember their child's birthday was because of medication used to induce amnesia during labor and to assist with pain management. "Twilight Sleep" was a combination of Demerol and Scopalamine. It was important to know what drugs were administered, because the trauma of surrendering a child at birth, combined with the drugs, could cause serious, if not psychotic, reactions to drugs later in life.

Dropping the book, I raced to read my hospital records, and sure enough, there it was listed. No wonder I couldn't remember anything - I was drugged, and against my will, knowledge or consent.

According to my hospital records, at 7:15 p.m. I was given my first dose of Demerol and Phenergan. Another drug, Seconal, was administered at 10:45 p.m. The next morning at 4:45, I was given Demerol, Phenergan and Scopalamine. At 8:45 a.m., I was again given Demerol and Scopalamine. At 10:10 a.m. glucose; at 11:45 a.m. and 1:20 p.m. just Demerol; at 3:30 p.m. both Demerol and Phenergan were again given together.

At 4:22 p.m. I was given a spinal and delivered an eight-pound baby girl by forceps. As many times as I had already read my hospital records, I had missed reading "the forceps had caused slight bruising on her left cheek, but there were no further abnormalities." My child had been damaged!

It was staggering to read how much I was drugged. My membrane had been ruptured, I had been cathetrized and given glucose, plus I had an episiotomy. And my daughter needed forceps to be delivered.

What had all this done to my child? In twenty-two hours, they had given me seven doses of drugs plus a spinal. At 3:00 p.m., I had been completely dilated, but did not deliver until almost an hour and a half later. Did my daughter not want to leave me?

After reading all this, I just finally had to call Peg back a few days later. She had good news for me. Apparently, the person born in 1961 with the same last name as my daughter was actually my daughter's sister. The contact was going to call her.

Elated to be getting so close, I was also apprehensive about how it would go. Peg reassured me. "We are in good hands," she said. "Don't worry, we are making progress."

The adoption files had stated that a second child had been adopted before the family visited the grandparents in Germany. If the sister was adopted in 1961, the law would have prohibited the family from taking the child out of the country for a full year, which meant my daughter had remained in the United States at least until she was three.

It was now November and I only had until Christmas to work with Peg. After that, I would have to petition the court again for an extra six months to be added to the search time.

My daily prayer was, "Please, God, may Bambi be alive and well."

The closer we came to making contact with my daughter, the more insecure I felt. Should I interfere with my daughter's life? Did I have the right to possibly disrupt a happy life? Was I being selfish, thinking only of myself? God, I had such doubts.

In dire need of shoring up at this point, I went to my Full Circle support group. As I spilled out my doubts to the group, one member said, "It's about time you became selfish. Take back your life!"

As I contemplated her words, I realized there was a great deal of truth to them. Up to this point, everyone else had told me what to do: my parents, my social worker, the birth father and society. It was just that I didn't want to hurt my child.

* * * * * * * *

Returning home and finding the house quiet, I decided to write a letter to Bambi. After being given permission for my feelings, I was suddenly feeling so close to her, and I needed to write down everything uncensored, so I could get my deepest feelings down.

With the doll perched on top of my computer stand looking down on me, my words poured out with such force, I didn't even need to edit the letter. It was as if I had been writing the letter for months. In reality, I had thought of little else.

After finishing the letter, I called Peg to see if she minded my reading it to her. Reassuring me that she felt confident we would find Bambi, she encouraged me to read the whole letter. Tears began flowing as soon as I began, and at first the words were hard to get out.

> Dear Daughter,
>
> I have to call you that because I don't know your new name. As a matter of fact, I don't know how to write this letter. What do you say to someone you gave birth to thirty-six years ago and have never seen? I guess the best way would be to introduce myself.
>
> My name is Sally and I am fifty-six years old, the mother of three sons and one daughter I have never met. Last year, I would have told people I had three sons. To have acknowledged you would have been too shameful. How could a mother give her own child away? I did that. Therefore, I could never, never have told anyone, as that would validate what a horrible person I was for doing such a thing. Then I attended an adoptee, birth parent and mental health convention in New York City, in the fall of 1994, and found out that it was okay for me to search for you.
>
> In order to search for you, I had to search for myself because, ever since giving you up, I gave part of me away. I lived through what other people wanted me to be, because I, for sure, couldn't be myself. I had messed up too much. While searching for myself, I found I am a strong person, capable of giving love and

because of circumstances beyond my control, had no other option but to relinquish you. Today that sounds so trite, what with welfare to aid mothers, and society not caring if you keep your child, married or not. In 1959, that was not the case.

Since I am an adoptee, I know the primal feeling of being given away. I have struggled with it all my life, wondering why my mother chose to dump me on a porch in a paper bag in the middle of the winter. Was I that bad? I have always wondered who I was. What was my medical background? Where do my genetic parts fit in? It felt like a circle was broken, a piece missing, which continually kept me off balance. I have been searching, for a year and a half now, for my parents. I need to know who they are. Where did I come from? When is my birthday?

Attending another adoption convention in New York City, I said during one session, that I didn't think I had the right to search for you. One young adopted daughter said, “I wish my mom would search for me! Search and don’t give up!” Her face comes to mind as I write this letter. Maybe you will want the same answers I have been searching for, too? You have always had a special place in my heart, but I never felt I had the right to know you. Giving you away was the biggest sin I have ever done. If I had only been given another option, I would have taken it.

Secrets tear people apart. My adopted family knew all about you, also my husband, but in all these years, no one has ever said a word about it. That is, until last year when I brought it up, telling everyone I was going to search for you. My strong desire to find you made my family realize this was something I had to do. It has taken me a long time to get to this point. I felt I had to find you to try to explain how this all came about.

You are the only daughter I have. It was like God made the best with you and then figured I didn't need any more daughters, so he gave me three wonderful sons. I know what it is like to have an adopted family.

They are your mom and dad. But I am also the other mother, the one that gave you life. I would love to meet you and have you meet your brothers. I also know you will need time to think about all of this.

I sincerely mean no harm to come to you. I am not here to interfere with your life. I just want at least one meeting with you, when you are ready, to explain it all. Before I close, I want to share with you a poem my new found, on-line computer friend Pam Silo wrote to her daughter. They have since been reunited. Pam sent it to me on a day I was having a terribly blue day from not being able to locate you.

It is called:

"In My Mind's Eye."

I did hold you to my breast and nurture you. When you cried, I ran to your side. I rocked you until your tears subsided.
When you were frightened, I held you until you were not frightened any longer.
I felt your first doctor's visit.
I was there. Your first shot, I could barely watch.
On your first day of school, I saw you walk to the door,
I saw you turn toward your mother.
I also gave you the little push you needed ... Did you feel it? You must have.
You knew it was going to be okay.
I saw you rush to your mother to tell her how great your first day of school was.
I saw your very first boyfriend....I know why you liked him....Puppy love was wonderful.
I scolded you when your grades weren't so good.
I was there to answer any question you felt the need to ask.
I kissed and bandaged you to make all your hurts go away.
Your first dance, did you know that we chose your dress together?

I thought it was beautiful. I took your picture.
Whenever you needed me, I was there...It's very hard to believe, I know.
My daughter, I loved you, I've loved you all these years...I love you today.
More than yesterday...I've longed for you.
I did want you. I did want to be your mother.
It just wasn't possible. It was not my choice.
Yes, yes my daughter. I was there...In My Mind's Eye.
It did not end for me after those wicked papers were signed.
I have not forgotten you.
I want to know that you are all right.
Now I must continue on.
My tears are lying in the dust.
I am a mother without her child...Gone from my sight, but not my mind.
No matter what is perceived, I am a mother who will continue to grieve.
For I am still a mother, no doubt. All you need is to look into my heart.
Now what do I do?
I hope and I pray, each and every day, that my daughter is safe and warm, protected and held, healthy and happy, loved and loved more every moment that passes.
The love in my heart is like no other...Simply because I am still……your mother.
I love you.

I cried so when I read Pam's poem, because it described exactly what I have had hidden deep inside me, but was afraid to say, all these years.

I will wait for your reply.

Love, Sally

"The letter is perfect," Peg said. "Don't change a thing."

That night, while taking the dog out before going to bed, I gazed up at the sky filled with brilliant stars and thought silently to myself that somewhere in this big world, under these beautiful stars, my daughter shares the same sky. May she feel my love and good thoughts whirling into space.

* * * * * * * *

As my feelings continued to erupt, despite all efforts, I sought new understanding, which I found in a book by the famous pediatrician T. Berry Brazelton, M.D. called *The Earliest Relationship*. In his chapter, 'The Dawn of Attachment,' he discussed the three stages of pregnancy. The first stage was the one that caught my attention.

> As the pregnant woman struggles through this turmoil of ambivalent emotions, she will be especially available to the support of others. An expectant mother often develops a strong transference to any supportive professional at this time. She yearns for understanding of her powerful emotions for mothering, as she prepares to be a mother.

It was clear to me that all my transference went to my social worker, as she was the only person I could talk to about my pregnancy. Such power I transferred to her without being conscious of why. When she said, "If you love your child, giving it to a loving, two parent family would be the best," I was too vulnerable not to believe her. After all, she was a mother herself and a professional.

But would my feelings have been different if I had loved the birth father? The circumstances of my daughter's conception were still difficult to feel comfortable thinking about. Just saying the word 'rape' caused me to flinch. Why didn't I seek emotional help back then? Why didn't I realize I had been raped? What caused me to think it was my fault all these years? Why did I continue to carry this terrible thing inside me, and why am I dealing with it at this particular time rather than at any other?

Back I went to the library to try to find answers. On a first name basis with the staff after my frequent visits, I was embarrassed for them to see the title I was checking out, *I Never Called It Rape*. What would they think about my investigating such a subject? Piling extra books on top for camouflage, I held my breath as I checked it out.

The house was quiet when I returned, so I curled up on the couch, finding my head nodding in agreement to so many of the words in front of me. The "Seven Victim Reactions After Being a Victim of an Acquaintance Rape," really spoke to me.

> #1. Denial: She denies this happened for the simple reason that she knew her attacker.
> #2. Dissociation: The woman during the rape feels physically and mentally removed from what is happening.
> #3. Self-Blame: Acquaintance rape victims feel betrayed by their own judgment that the man they chose to be with turned on them.
> #4. Victim Reaction: We all have an inner 'Little Voice' that can sense danger and sends out a warning signal.
> #5. No fighting Back: After being raped, many victims are angry with themselves for not fighting back harder even though, at the time of the rape, most report feeling afraid for their lives.
> #6. Not reporting the attack: Many women, victims of acquaintance rape don't report their experience because they don't think the police or anyone else will believe them.
> #7. Becoming a victim again: 42% of women who were raped said they had sex again with the man who assaulted them. 55% of the men who raped said they had sex again with their victims. Why? The answer lay in the confusion that date rape and acquaintance rape

> victims feel about the rape. "'I must have misunderstood him." "I didn't make myself clear." "I'm wrong for feeling bad about this."

Amazingly, "84% of the men who committed rape said what they did was definitely not rape." My daughter's father had asked me why I fought so hard. He never believed he had done anything wrong.

Even with this validation, I was still reluctant to call it rape, believing there had to be a weapon involved for it to be real rape. There had to be a gun or a knife. In her book, *Taking Back My Life*, Nancy Ziegenmeyer, the first woman to go public about her own rape explained:

> Stranger rape is the use of sex to get power over the victim; acquaintance rape is the use of power to get sex. If the acquaintance or date wants to have sex with you and you do not want to have sex with him, and you say no, and he ignores you, or pretends he doesn't hear you, or he overrules you, or he doesn't give a damn about what you're saying at that point and goes ahead anyway; you've been raped.

Closing the book, I felt sick. Clutching my stomach, I slowly climbed the stairs and crawled into bed. Curling up into a fetal position, I grabbed the heating pad, hoping to ease my pain, and started talking out loud to myself. "This is crazy, Sally. This happened thirty-six years ago. You now know why you denied this event happened. You now know why you dissociated yourself from the situation. God knows, you might have cracked up. So why are you still blaming yourself? Why are you having such a stomachache?

Then the shocking answer came. For the first time since the rape happened, I was feeling angry. Really angry! Screaming primal sounds and beating my pillow, I was grateful that no one was around to hear me. Banging away,

I thought that because of one person's violent act, my life was changed forever. Not just my life, but my daughter's life and my family's life, too.

Amazingly, I still had to convince myself and found myself yelling out loud to an empty room, "I now know it was not my fault! It was not my fault!" Why did I still need to pound this fact into my brain?

*   *   *   *   *   *   *   *

Books I had requested from the library on the subject of attachment were stacked on my dining room table. Could a woman other than a child's natural mother honestly fill the role of attachment figure? My hopes were to find the answer to be, 'No,' because of my own mothering experience. But the author of *Attachment: Loss Disorder* said, "Yes. Almost from the first, many children have more than one figure towards whom they direct attachment behavior; these figures are not treated alike, the role of a child's principal attachment-figure can be filled by others than the natural mother."

My consolation was that my daughter was indeed able to attach to her adoptive parents. Comfort from that thought was brief, as I read the results of author John Bolby's research.

> Though there can be no doubt that a substitute mother can behave in a completely mothering way to a child, and that many do so, it may well be less easy for a substitute mother than for a natural mother to do so. For example, knowledge of what elicits mothering behavior in other species suggests that hormonal levels following parturition and stimuli emanating from the newborn baby himself may be of great importance. If this is so for human mothers also, a substitute mother must be at a disadvantage compared with a natural mother. Therefore, a substitute's mothering responses

> may well be less strong to less consistently elicited than those of a natural mother.

So if this were true, then what did my daughter's substitute mothering do to her? Was my child able to sense it wasn't me?

Bolby's next title matched my mood - *Attachment: Loss, Sadness and Depression*. In it he stated, "When attachment and loss causes sadness and depression, the responses to loss seen in early life have a great deal in common with responses seen in later life."

Perhaps this was one of the reasons I cried out when my father died that I was now all alone in the world. At the time, I could not imagine where such an outburst originated. The words just erupted from my soul. When others had tried to comfort me, deep down I knew it was not possible. With both my adoptive parents gone, I was again an orphan.

Bowlby quoted Sigmund Freud:

> Although we know that after a loss the acute state of mourning will subside, we also know we shall remain inconsolable and will never find a substitute. No matter what may fill the gap, even if it be filled completely, it nevertheless remains something else. And actually this is how it should be. It is the only way of perpetuating that love which we do not want to relinquish.

Was this why so many adoptees have this deep inner longing to find their lost mother? All their substitutions could never hope to fill the void.

On the other hand, the authors of *Bonding-Building the Foundations of Secure Attachment and Independence* felt that attachment was altogether absent at birth and not strongly in evidence until after an infant was past the sixth month. But what happened during the first six months then. What happens right after birth?

Back to at the library for more research, I discovered *The Amazing Newborn.* I myself was amazed to learn things new to me despite the fact I had given birth to four children. This was way beyond Dr. Spock. Certain passages just stunned me.

> For the first forty-three minutes, in the quiet alert stage, when the infant's eyes are wide open, they are able to respond to their environment. If allowed and covered warmly, and placed on the mother's stomach, the baby will first rest, look around, their eyes directed to the sound of their mother's voice. Soon they will crawl up the mother's stomach and find the breast.
>
> When the infants are skin-to-skin with their mothers, for the first ninety minutes, they cry hardly at all, compared to infants who were wrapped in a towel and placed in a bassinet.
>
> A mother and child, during those first few days after the baby is born, are especially suited to each other physiologically, hormonally and emotionally. Because of the *Bonding-Building the Foundations of Secure Attachment and Independence* authors research, we believe that there is firm evidence for the benefits of early contact between parents and infants immediately after birth.
>
> The mothers who miss out are often those at the limits of adaptability and who stand to benefit the most - the poor, the single, the unsupported and the teenage mothers.

With horror, I imagined my baby's reality just after delivery, crying off in the distance, not being allowed to be comforted by me. If the research was correct, I had done great damage to my child's psyche, now knowing just how much my daughter needed me. Breaking our connection was cruel!

> Both mothers and babies can find each other through the sense of smell. A mother can pick out her infant among other infants through smell within the first day after having had only one hour of contact. The mother senses the baby at many different levels. The whole system appears to enable the mother to communicate with her infant in ways that can bypass the logical and rational areas of the brain and allow the mother to take in and sense the baby at a deeper, more primitive level.

Finally, I got it! Bonding had to do with things on a primal level of being. This sounded like the perfect argument for keeping families together whenever possible. After all these years, I still ached to have had those first few days with my child, to have had her lie on my stomach, to have been allowed to have quieted her infant's fears after such a traumatic birth. No adoptive mother could have the birth mother's familiar smell, touch, or familiar voice.

Reubon Pannor was right. I had attached to my adoptive parents as they took care of my every need as an infant. But, what was missing was my own learned, in utero natural instincts allowing bonding with my natural mother. No wonder separation from her felt like an amputation. In families kept intact, bonding happens and so does attachment. In adoption this is not the case because there can only be an attachment.

* * * * * * * *

My mind tried to find a way to make my daughter's adoption illegal. Twenty-one was the age of majority in Michigan, and when I signed the papers I was only twenty. I had no legal guardian. How did all the parties involved get around this point? Did living alone qualify me? Had the social worker become my legal guardian without my knowing it?

CHAPTER NINE

So many questions I had. Finally, I forced myself to put them all aside and start dinner. But stirring ground beef for spaghetti sauce was not engaging enough to fill my mind, and I found myself going over all the events of the year long search for my daughter. Would I ever find her?

Later that night, while wrapping holiday gifts, I saw from the reflection through the window that there was a full moon outside. Peg had always said she had the most luck with searches during the time of a full moon, so I decided to give her a call. We hadn't spoken in a few weeks. Perhaps there was something new to report.

But the news that Peg had to report was disturbing. Apparently, she had tried to reach me on Monday, though there was no message from her on the machine, and when she didn't get a hold of me took matters into her own hands. Together with Mary, the social worker, they decided to write directly to the adoptive parents to get my daughter's married name and address.

I could not believe what I was hearing. My body went into shock and my mind became scattered, unable to focus. I was frozen in fear. But, somehow my inner voice spoke loud and clear. Listen to your emotions. Think with your head, but pay attention to how you really feel for a change. What do you want?

Calmly, but in a strong, firm voice I reminded Peg that I had said no to the same idea when she had suggested we contact the father through Social Security. I thought I had made it clear that I wanted to contact my daughter directly.

The more I spoke, the more upset I became as it sank in that they had decided to write a letter to the adoptive parents behind my back. It was not what I had agreed to when I hired Peg, and I didn't want the letter sent.

Peg said very slowly, "Well, I will call Mary and tell her your wishes. The reason our Amsterdam contact didn't contact your daughter's sister is because she just found out she has terminal cancer and doesn't want to deal with this anymore. "I will call you right back."

Dejected, I hung up the phone. It was certainly understandable that the searcher in Holland no longer wished to help, but to contact the parents? Fear gripped me as I continued wrapping gifts while waiting for Peg's return call.

Twenty minutes later, Peg called back with the news that the letter had already been sent. Trying to appease me, Peg said the letter had been written very professionally in English and in Dutch. She would send me a copy. "The deadline given the adoptive parents to respond with your daughter's married name and address," Peg said, "was made for December twenty-eighth."

They gave the adoptive parents a deadline! All they would have to do is deny ever having received the letter and the search for my child would be over. They will think I am trying to take their child away. Now the letter I wrote to Bambi seemed all for naught. In the midst of my turmoil, I realized that I was stuck. If I fired Peg, I would be left with nothing. She had all my daughter's information.

Bringing my attention back to the conversation, I heard Peg saying, "I felt our time was running out and we needed to do something now, as you were being kept in limbo." But I had to wonder if the real looming deadline was actually December twenty-second, when the time allotted by the court for Peg to search was up.

"I hope the adage that nothing is ever an accident holds true in this case," I told her.

Since I already had her on the phone, I asked Peg about my idea that my daughter's adoption was not actually legal since I had no legal guardian at the time of signing the relinquishment papers. If I could find a crack in the system, perhaps I could eliminate the need for a searcher. But Peg assured me that, when I went through the agency, they became my legal guardian. How could they be when I was never told that? Now I was doubly angry!

As I hung the phone back up I felt choked: wanting to cry but unable, wanting to scream but couldn't.

As I resumed my project of wrapping the gifts, I popped the cassette of a workshop that I had missed at the adoption conference into the tape recorder. With the same synchronicity that always seemed to accompany my search, the speaker talked about feeling the moment, warning not to shut down.

What I was feeling was rage and I had no idea what to do with it. Gathering the courage to dump it all onto my friends online, I was rewarded with their insights. The way they explained it that made perfect sense was that I was thrown back to the memories and feelings of being nineteen-years-old again and in the situation of dealing with the all controlling social worker at the agency. The searcher was now playing the same controlling role. Did my feelings or requests count? No! This matter had been taken out of my hands and I was now at the mercy of the searcher just as I had been at the mercy of the social worker thirty-five years before. This time, I had the opportunity to do things differently.

But then trying to think positively, I thought that maybe Christmas was the best time for this letter to arrive at the adoptive parents' house. Maybe my daughter will come home for the holidays and they will tell her I'm looking for her. But then, getting worried again, I thought she could be dead and that was why she couldn't be found.

Not having any answers just tortured my mind. How was I ever going to get through the holidays in an upbeat mood? I needed to pay attention to my family when all I wanted to do was scream. Feeling I had to put my feelings aside for my family's sake, I installed my "perfect mother tape" and gave the performance of my life.

* * * * * * * *

Within a few days, I received a copy of the letter the social worker had sent to the adoptive family, dated December 5, 1995. It read:

> Dear _____,
>
> May I introduce myself. I am a sixty-year old married pastor's wife as well as a Family therapist who has resided in the USA the past 40 years. I am also an adoptee who works a lot with families who have had an adoption experience. Three years ago I discovered two half-brothers and a sister in the Netherlands. I'm still in contact with one of them. The other two would rather not and I recognize their rights of freedom of choice. All our parents have since passed away and my only regret is that I did not meet them while living.
>
> My husband and I are parents of three married children and grandparents to three little boys and a two-year-old girl. When my pregnant daughter heard in 1992 that I had just seen a picture of my birth father for the first time, she wanted to know all about it, especially the medical information which was important to her.
>
> Now the actual reason for my writing to you. Last October I was at an Adoption Conference in New York City. There in a workshop I met a woman from California who was about 55 years of age. She had heard the story about my search in the Netherlands. She told me that at age 20 she released a child for adoption at the Detroit Women's Hospital. The baby

was born on 10-27-59 and the birth mom named her Bambi Lynn (the mother was an airline hostess at the time). She does not know who adopted her baby but she was told by her court appointed intermediary that her 35 year-old daughter lived in the Netherlands since the early 60's. I did not get to spend much time with this woman, but gave her my business card and agreed to be willing to be contacted by her intermediary.

Peg Richards, the director of Aim, has since called me several times. She was appointed by the court to work on the birth mother's behalf. She has worked on this case for almost six months and is asking for my help because the Dutch language and customs are unknown to her.

Our question to you is this: Would you be so kind as to give us the married name (if applicable) and current address of (THE NAME WAS CUT OUT MAKING A HOLE IN THE PAPER), your oldest daughter. We understand that this may be difficult for you because often there is a fear that the birth mother might become intrusive and this can give a feeling of loss. I can reassure you, however, that this birth mother struck me as very rational, mature and well-balanced.

It has been my professional experience that most family reunions are motivated by a need to verify that the other is really alright, that the birth parent made the right decision when she was young, so that she can stop the self-blame and can gain some inner peace at this stage in the lifespan.

We look forward to your affirmative answer no later than December 28, 1995. By the first week of January, this case will be transferred to a new intermediary who will continue the search on her own, if need be. You can reach me at the enclosed address or preferably by fax.

Sincerely,
_____MSW: ACSW
Licensed Marriage and Family Therapist

The letter had been sent December 5, and I had not reached Peg until December 8. So, it was obvious the letter had already been sent when I called Peg, and there was nothing I could have done about it. I continued to feel very uneasy.

The part explaining about all the birth mother's need to know, to find peace, just didn't feel right. I doubted I would ever have inner peace.

*   *   *   *   *   *   *   *

Abruptly, I was temporarily pulled back into the search for my birth parents. The York Hospital librarian, Diane Robinson, sent the student nurses yearbook for the Class of 1939, thinking I might like to photo copy the picture of the student nurse holding me in front of the rest of the classmates. After photocopying all the graduating nurses who had tended to me while I awaited adoption, I put the yearbook aside. It was just too much to deal with on top of reeling from the letter being sent to my daughter's parents behind my back. I felt helpless.

My oldest son, Jay, suggested I write my own letter to the adoptive family to put their mind at ease. Unfortunately, that was impossible since only the searcher had their name and address.

My youngest son, Daniel, suggested I needed to get my control back. "There is only one way to do it, Mom," he said. "You need to take care of yourself. You can't allow the system to destroy you."

Their encouragement helped me feel better, but I was really emotionally too numb to act. Staring at the hole in the paper where my daughter's adoptive names had been cut out was such an insult and seemed to symbolize what was wrong with the entire adoption/birth parent situation. Everything had to be a secret. But why, really? Did they think I might actually harm my own child? The hole seemed to say, “Sally, you are bad. You are a scorned woman. You are entitled to nothing. You gave her up!”

My anger finally gave me the energy to take the search into my own hands. There were a couple of things I knew: two listings were under the parents’ phone number; and the parents had a common American last name. Asking my husband’s help, he called contacts that promised to send a phone book from Amsterdam. My plan was to go through the entire phone book and write down every American name having two listings. No matter how long it took, I would call each number until I found my daughter.

While waiting for the phone book to arrive, I hooked up with Internet news groups in Holland at the suggestion of an online friend Reenie, who gave me instructions on how to go about it.

From the non-identifying information, I knew that the adoptive father had a technical job and was also retired. So, I posted an inquiry about retired employees from IBM, knowing they had an office in Amsterdam. Perhaps the father had worked there.

Not expecting anything, I was surprised to hear from a man named Chris, who had just retired from IBM.

My angels were at work again!

Chris wanted to know how he could help, and I told him how I was looking for my daughter and needed to find her last name, that my searcher wouldn’t give it to me. Since I believe it was highly likely that the adoptive father had worked for IBM, I asked Chris to see if he could find out if anyone retired having an American name. Then if he could be on hand to answer any questions that might arise, I would be forever grateful. With his promise for help, I jumped for joy. I had made a new friend.

* * * * * * * *

In the midst of baking holiday cookies and reflecting over the news that Chris's search of retired IBM employees had produced no results, the doorbell rang. Wiping the dough from my hands, I opened the door to find the postman delivering my Christmas/Chanukah present from my sister-in-law. Even though I already knew what was in it, I tore open the box too excited to wait until December 25th. It was my Dorothy from the Wizard of Oz doll, the one I had seen in the country store with my sister-in-law while on a searching trip for clues to finding my mother. The doll had screamed out for me to take it home, but my sister-in-law grabbed it from me saying she was going to give it to me for Christmas.

As I examined the doll, I wondered if my strong feelings were because Dorothy was also an orphan. Or, was it because the movie was released the year I was born? Feeling there had to be something more to the affinity I felt, I went straight to the library the next day.

Sitting down in the library and reading the original story, the connection became clear. Our lives actually paralleled each other's. Dorothy continually searched for information about her natural mother, just like I was doing. Then, while searching, Dorothy discovered her father had been an older man, a teacher at her mother's school. My exact story! Dorothy's birth, like mine, was kept a secret. Wanting the doll to be a prominent part of the family celebrations, I propped Dorothy up against the back of my velvet chair in the living room.

* * * * * * * *

With the New Year's celebrations over, I was again off to volunteer at Women Helping Women, a center supporting abused women, but before leaving, I checked our bookshelves to see if we had any travel books on Mexico. Ross wanted to take me away there to relax, and I wanted to find out what the temperatures there would be so I'd know what clothes to pack.

What I ran across instead was a book on Holland. When had I bought this? Was discovering it a sign of something to come?

Sure enough, when I returned home, there was a fax waiting for me. Its cover letter was from the social worker in Holland, Michigan. Glancing over it, I realized it was a letter from the adoptive parents.

With my heart pounding in my ears, I slid into the nearest chair and laid the fax down on the table until I could gather myself enough to fully concentrate on the letter. Finally, all my attention was on the piece of paper in front of me. After thirty-five years, I was about to receive real information concerning my child. The realization was overwhelming. As excited as I was, I was also afraid, suddenly certain she didn't want to meet me.

Very slowly, I peaked at the letter. It was dated December 15, 1995. Now curious, I read on.

Dear ______,

We received your letter regarding our eldest daughter. I am rather amazed that you assume we would release her address to you without her consent. She is a very talented woman living a full and joyous life and quite capable of making her own decisions, certainly in a matter as important to her as this one.

She is about to give birth and I will give her your letter when she has fully recovered and she and her new baby are doing well.

She can then decide for herself if she wants to respond. I think it is wholly up to her and all concerned should await her decision.

We still are quite often in Michigan and I have given her all information regarding AIM a few years ago upon returning from one of our trips. She had no interest. Please respect our privacy and wait whether she responds or not.

Sincerely,
(Blacked out name)

She is talented, living a joyous, happy life and having a baby! I was so pleased to know all that. At the same time, a horribly negative thought came into my mind that she probably wouldn't be this talented and joyous if she had been raised by me.

But it was the words, "Our daughter has no interest in searching for her birth mother," that made me feel like I had been knocked to the ground, bruised and bloody.

Here I was, intruding on her happy, joyous life. At least that was what it seemed her parents felt I was doing. Never, ever had I intruded on anyone's life before, and this feeling was uncomfortable. Their letter made me out to be the bad party, and I had no way of letting them know my intentions were honorable.

Why did the adoptive mother's comments bother me so much? I should be happy. My daughter was alive! She had been told she was adopted. And, I was about to be a grandmother. Well, I wasn't joyous. I actually hated the letter for making me feel I counted for so little in their eyes.

When I handed the letter to Ross, he laid it back down on the table after reading it and said, "Sally, I think you missed something. The social worker gave you your daughter's name."

Stunned, I reread the letter and sure enough, there it was - Ludia. How in the world had I missed it? After all these years, I finally knew her name! Ludia. It was different, like the searcher said. Ludia. It sounded so foreign, so Dutch or German. Not like the American girl she really was.

The cover letter from the social worker read:

Dear Sally,

I don't feel it is a bad letter. I expected some anger at the intrusion. It must seem incredible to them that AIM has traced them down this far. Once you look beyond this resentment, you will notice that they are open to daughter's search and are sincere (I believe) in being willing to pass on your letter to her after the birth of her (1st ?) baby.

They would not have had to share this information, that is why I think they are sincere. No mention is made of a husband, which makes me wonder if she is a single mom. Individual rights and privacy rights are very strong in Western Europe. You also know that the adoptee needs to consent before any identifying information is released. The ball is now in Ludia's court. (There was the name!) I am confident that the adoptive parents will cooperate and leave her the choice, when she is ready.

* * * * * * * *

Thank God for my online friends. I went straight to my computer to get a different perspective from the one I was developing. They pointed out that my daughter was not the one to say that she didn't want to meet me. It was the adoptive mother that wanted to say it. Apparently it was quite common and very natural that, not wanting to upset the adoptive parents, the child will say they do not want to search, yet when found are thrilled. It seemed my daughter's adoptive mother was being protective, perhaps unnecessarily yet understandably so. On the one hand, she said their daughter was perfectly capable of making her own decisions, then on the other hand was wanting to wait until she felt it was appropriate, concerned about the impact as she was soon to deliver a baby.

For myself I was torn in two as both sides of my adoption experience crashed together, making everything hard to understand. My birth mother feelings wanted immediate and direct contact with my daughter, while my adoptee feelings wanted to comfort the adoptive family. I wanted them to know I was an honorable person. And I was also resentful. Why couldn't they give Ludia the letter now?

Pulled in different directions, I became deeply depressed. Conflicting emotions of rejection, loss, happiness and confusion warred within me. Why was I setting myself up for rejection? This must be such a primal desire to want something so badly that I could be willing to face any amount of pain and fear for it.

All I knew for certain was that I had to send the letter I had written to Ludia months before. From everything I had read, and what I knew in my heart to be true, the first letter one's child reads needs to be one they can treasure. Ludia couldn't treasure the letter from the social worker. It was addressed to the adoptive parents and not to her. And it wasn't from me.

Immediately phoning Peg, I practically demanded that she send my letter right away and ask the adoptive parents to substitute it for social worker's letter when they fulfilled their promise. If I were to have any chance of meeting her, she had to read my letter. If, after reading mine, she did not want to meet me, it would be easier to live with. I would understand. My son, Daniel, was right. I felt much better taking control back.

* * * * * * * *

Happy to be going on vacation, I threw the book *Synchronicity and Reunion* into my carry-on and then thought to check my email one more time before leaving for the airport. One of my birth mother friends said, "You are grieving the loss of your daughter, something most of us never do until we are reunited." This felt right. Just knowing Ludia was the only female in my life carrying my genetic make-up was intensifying my loss, not to mention the fact that she would soon deliver a new generation from the female line of my family. That understanding was visceral.

Letting my mind wonder on the flight down to Mexico, I remembered a statement in *Nature's Thumb Print*, which read, "Examine each life for its surface meaning and you will see strands by the thousands. Look backward and see a childhood of parental influence, but still further back to find generations of inherited connections. We are bound to the strands that lead us back, as we are bound to tradition." What was my unknown past and my daughter's inherited connection? Did Ludia work for an airline like I did? Or was she involved in something more on the creative side? Who knew? She could be an anchor person on television. When, if ever, would I have answers to my endless questions?

Our private villa was very isolated and I was happy I had brought a lot to read. After trying to play tennis and climbing four hundred stairs to the beach and back, I wanted nothing more that to sit in the sun and read.

Choosing first *Synchronicity and Reunion*, I read about a study done by Dudrear (1991). It said: "Reunited birth mothers from a variety of religions experienced a crises of faith because of their adoption separation. Their communication with God became direct rather than through an intermediary or priest."

Gazing out over the beautiful blue water, I vividly recalled desperately searching for a church to help mend my wounded soul, a soul void of my daughter and my first mother. Every Sunday morning, dressed in my best church clothes, I would stand at a Detroit bus stop, waiting to be taken to the church I had circled on my city map the night before. Often times, passing motorists would solicit my services, believing that was why I was standing on a street corner alone.

This practice went on for weeks. But, none of the churches I attended felt right to me. After my quest throughout the city, I discovered the large Methodist Church, just a block from my apartment, was the one that felt most like home and I became a member. It was there that I had the incredible privilege of hearing Martin Luther King preach.

Four days into our vacation, while everyone went swimming, played tennis or cards, I began to write. As I filled page after page, answers began to emerge.

Reading back what I had written, tears streamed down my cheeks because I finally understood what had been upsetting me. Receiving the letter from Ludia's parents touched a pocket of feelings stored from the time I had signed the relinquishment papers. As my online friend has said, I was grieving, something I had never allowed myself to do. My daughter is alive and I must grieve –a strange and confusing feeling.

Just as Lavonne Stiffler, author of *Synchronicity and Reunion*, said, "A birth mother may not feel her grief initially, but it will surface later in her life, perhaps at reunion or at the birth of a grandchild. She might not start grieving until as many as forty years later." For me it had taken thirty-five years to begin to feel the all-encompassing pain.

* * * * * * * *

After returning home, I faced putting away all the holiday decorations. Busy working on the project, a beep from the machine let me know that a fax was coming in. The news was not good. It was from the social worker informing me that the adoptive family had hired an attorney to make sure that the searcher and the social worker did not contact Ludia until the family felt it was time. Part of the social workers fax read: "I received a letter from the side of the authorities in the Netherlands. If I press too much, I could be considered overstepping privacy boundaries. In a way you can understand that the adoptive parents are least eager to share their first grand parenting experience."

But I was shocked that they felt they had to hire an attorney to keep me away from my adult daughter. I couldn't believe it!

Immediately, I called Peg. After hearing the actual letter from the attorney, I felt relieved. It was nothing more than a simple form letter that attorneys send to scare people. The trouble was, Peg and the social worker were taking it to heart, saying they would obey the demand. Obviously they could no longer help me, and I was on my own feeling very much abandoned, no longer with anyone to hold my hand through the process.

Again, my mind was split. On the one hand, I felt I could trust the adoptive parents to give Ludia the letter. Yet, on the other hand, I felt I needed to continue to search on my own. Why should I believe the adoptive family? My common sense was saying one thing, my emotions another, creating nothing but gibberish.

Any efforts I made to search on my own behalf were to no avail. Everything seemed out of my hands. My options having run out and my utter helplessness caused everything I saw on television to make me cry and my stomach to hurt. Holland was so far away. Finally, I went to bed, pulled the covers over my head and declared, "The heck with the world. I can't take anymore."

As I lay in bed, my stomach painfully cramping, I thought to myself that I should be happy knowing Ludia was alive and about to have a baby. But, I wasn't. All I could feel was the kick to my gut from her adoptive mom's statement that my daughter had no interest in finding me.

But then, perhaps my stomach was aching in sympathy with my daughter, who might be in labor at this very moment.

CHAPTER TEN

It was now the end of January, a year since beginning the search for my daughter. And it was the day I celebrated my birthday. As my consciousness grew, the longer I searched for my daughter and for my parents, the more the fact that I didn't really know for certain what my birth date really was made celebrating any of the possible dates feel fake. Officially, I arbitrarily observed it on January 29. But it felt like a sham.

Hoping shopping would lift my depression, I found myself wandering up and down the aisles at Cost Plus. Passing by a shelf of cocktail napkins depicting countries of the world, the one from Holland immediately caught my eye. I didn't need them, but, in a strange way, they made me feel a little closer to Ludia.

As always when my birthday was over, my depression would lift, as if by some miracle. Feeling better, I was determined to exercise, eat right and forget about searching.

But, almost the instant I made my resolution, the phone rang. It was Peg. "I have good news," she said. "I have heard from your daughter!"

My thought was, after all we had been through, this must be some kind of joke. Peg probably heard through a lawyer, or the adoptive parents were telling us to back off again. "This must be a joke!" I said to Peg.

"I don't joke about such things," was Peg's stern reply. "Ludia said to release all her identifying information to you."

My world came to a screeching halt.

Peg continued, “ I can’t give you this information until I have Ludia sign the court issued ‘Release of Information’ form.”

Not wanting to miss a word she said, I held the phone so tightly to my ear that it physically hurt. I heard her say, “I will mail this form to her to sign. Then, when it is returned, I have to file it with the court. Then, when I hear from the court, I will give you all her information.”

My daughter wanted to meet me! Just knowing this was enough to release what felt like a thick liquid healing energy through my body, creating a stillness I was not familiar with. Immersed in the peace, I had to remember to focus on the conversation. Peg was saying, “ Ludia also sent a personal letter to you. Would you like me to open it and read it to you?”

By now, tears of joy were streaming down my face. “Yes!” was all I could manage. So afraid I wouldn’t remember all that was said, I grabbed a scrap of paper and wrote down everything.

My daughter had been shocked and happy to receive my letter. She lives in Amsterdam and has two daughters, ages two years and four months and one who was three weeks old the day she wrote the letter. She grew up in an American, German, Dutch family. There were four children. Two were adopted and two were biological. She was the oldest. Her family moved to Holland in 1965. She was a college graduate and a journalist. She was not married, but lived with the father of her two girls. Her letter was dated January 29, 1996, the date I celebrate my birthday. Maybe she had been writing it at the same exact time I was buying those cocktail napkins!

Her letter went on to say that, while meeting would be both scary and risky for us both, it was something she wanted to do. She did not hold it against me for letting her be adopted.

As Peg finished, all that stayed with me was that she did not hold it against me, and that she wanted to meet.

Bursting to tell everyone, I thanked Peg and told her I just had to hang up.

I told Ross first, then left messages for the others as no one was home. Overwhelmed with happiness I just had to release somehow. I got onto the Internet and wrote to all my online birth mother friends who had been so supportive.

Soon, the phone started ringing. My oldest son Jay was happy for me. My youngest, Dan, offered that the reason I was feeling weepy was not just from the happiness, but also because I finally met my goal and now everything, all the tension was releasing. Kiley was traveling, so we were out of touch. Ross said tonight I would finally be able to sleep!

My sister asked what my feelings were at the moment. All I felt was gratitude - grateful that Ludia did not hold what I did against me, grateful she wanted to meet, and gratitude to her adoptive parents for giving her the letter. For some reason, too, I wanted to make an appointment with a plastic surgeon. Maybe it was from a deep need for Ludia to know me as I was when we were still together.

* * * * * * * *

Ross was right. For the first time in a year, I slept through the night. I didn't even dream. After the initial shock of the wonderful news, I awoke feeling excited, thrilled, happy and on top of the world. From the rooftops, I wanted to shout at the top of my lungs, "I found my daughter and she wants to meet me!" Oh, such joy. I could not have been pumped up any higher.

My happiness permeated every facet of my life. Everywhere I went I told people that I had found my daughter: the waitresses where I had coffee, my hair dresser, the grocery checker, the bookkeeper at the chiropractor's office, the gardener and anyone else who would listen heard the story of my good fortune.

Especially meaningful was telling the grocery clerk who surprised me with her story of just recently reuniting with her thirty-year-old daughter who had looked for her. As I wrote my check out for the groceries, Anita and I reminisced about our daughters, the incessant beeping of the register only slightly intruding on our conversation. After exchanging big hugs, I pushed the cart out to the car. Not until I reached home did I realize why the register would not stop beeping. I still had the large check I had made out in my wallet. Returning the check the next day, I literally skipped out of the grocery store, thrilled to have connected with another birth mother.

So, what happened next was completely unexpected. My joy lasted for only a few days, and then the tears began to flow again. I could not imagine what was happening to me when I was so happy. Was I losing my mind?

I wasn't even certain my friends online would understand, but I had to try explaining this strange reaction to them.

Subject: If I Am So Happy, Why Am I Crying?
Date: 96-02-07
From: SJH
To: Birth Mother List.com

Dear Ladies,

I am not higher than a kite, like some of you said I would be. In fact, I have a stomachache. Kind words are producing tears. Finding Ludia, on the one hand has me exhilarated. On the other hand, not finding my mother is making me sad.

All I want to do is be able to share myself with my daughter, so she in turn can know herself better. Does that make sense? This is something I knew I had to do before I die.

The fact that Ludia doesn't hate me scares me. Everything I have read, and what I have heard at adoption conventions has led me to believe I should EXPECT MY CHILD TO BE ANGRY. Yet, I don't think I would be angry at my birth mom if I found her. Then people tell me I am not facing my REAL feelings. Everything in this reunion touches my own inability to find my birth parents and as my husband said, "You have like ping pong balls bouncing back and forth inside you."

While I should be on cloud nine, I am so down. Maybe I need therapy because I don't have a clue what is going on. I never knew I had so many people that loved me and are supporting me in this, so then why am I sad??

I am also scared to death about meeting her. I, the adoptee, want it to be perfect and fear it might not be. Now I know this is stupid talk, as things just happen, but old trends are hard to break. I would love some feedback on why I am so sad, grateful and not higher than a kite, but telling everyone I meet I have a daughter who wants to meet me.

Sally

Every e-mail answer said they had experienced great tears in their reunion/post reunion period, too. While all their advice was reassuring, I still was unable to get over the weepy stage and did not like it one bit.

When this stage persisted, my support group leader at Full Circle, Cindy, directed me to a birth mother therapist. By the time the appointment came, I hesitated going since I was beginning to feel better. But I went anyway, and found it very helpful in understanding myself.

Dr. Mantecon said that our emotions at reunion are like a spiral. Immediately, my own mind took over. The image of the spiral became a spring inside me. The spring was 'V' shaped, graduating in size. The narrow part was hooked to my pelvis and the wide part attached to the top of my ribs. The largest loop permeated my entire stomach. Now, it was like the spring had sprung loose and was bouncing back and forth, keeping me off kilter.

All those years, the spring had actually been coiled tightly. Neat. Tidy. Controlled. Now the spring was sprung! The emotions whirling around inside the spiral were like particles sucked up into a tornado. “If I am feeling this much pain,” I told the therapist “maybe I shouldn’t have searched?”

“The pain was inside you anyway,” Dr. Mantecon responded.

That this kind of pain was inside me was news to me.

* * * * * * * *

Waiting to receive Ludia’s letter from Peg was driving me crazy. So, to kill time, I thought I would write my daughter a letter of reply, so it would be ready to go. When I called Peg to see how Ludia signed her name, I learned she went by the name Liddie.

Sitting at my computer, I typed in “Dear Liddie.” But, that’s all that came. Tearing up page after page in frustration, I wondered why I was having such a hard time finding the right words.

A few days later, I tried again. But the only words that came from me were, “Liddie, Liddie, I am so giddy!” And that would never do! Writing a letter to my daughter seemed an impossible task.

* * * * * * * *

Again I was not sleeping well, frustrated and impatient to receive Liddie’s letter. One night I was startled awake. It felt like something had shaken my bed. Sitting up, I found myself looking at a vision at the foot of my bed. After hearing enough stories from others who had similar experiences, I knew to trust that what I was seeing was real, sort of. Not afraid, I concentrated hard on what I was seeing.

What I saw was a large dark circle, the size of a hula hoop, which was like nothing I had ever seen before. The vision overpowered me, taunting me to figure out its symbolism. Grabbing a pad of paper from my nightstand, I started drawing a perfect circle, black in the middle, so black I could not see through to the other side.

Peering up from the paper, I sensed the vision wanted me to step into its flat dark space, to experience the unknown it offered, the pain, happiness and excitement it held within. It seemed to promise that if I did, I would find peace, light and understanding on the other side.

But, I was not about to walk through the black, flat, unknown space. It was far too scary. Pinching myself to make sure I wasn't dreaming, I pulled the covers over my head and went back to sleep. This was all just nutty stuff.

But, then waking up the next morning, it all made sense. The vision represented the birth canal. I was about to give birth to my daughter all over again. This time, I vowed, no one would ever come between us. This reunion will be our journey alone, together.

* * * * * * * *

Grabbing a box of Kleenex from my therapist's desk, I pondered out loud whether to call or to write first. My fear about calling was that I would start crying and not stop. Then my daughter would think I was crazy.

Dr. Mantecon assured me, "Anything you do will come from your heart, and it will be normal, not crazy."

I decided it would be more comfortable to write. Writing came more naturally to me.

But why was her letter taking so long to arrive? This was torture. A livid Peg called with the answer.

"The court returned Liddie's SIGNED consent form stating it was not completed in full. It seems Liddie did not include the name of her adoptive mother and father, and I missed it."

The court knew the name of her parents, so why was it so important for Liddie to name them? She was an adult not a child. Now it would most likely take two months to receive the letter, one month to have Liddie receive the form and send it back and another for the court to process it again. Had Liddie, too, felt it unnecessary to name her parents and so was making a statement? Or was it an oversight?

Since my time was about to expire with the court appointed searcher, would that mean further delays while I was appointed another?

I stomped around the house, my fury in full bloom. For once, I was not going to rationalize my anger away. This whole search process was ridiculous! My grown daughter, a consenting adult, wants to meet the mother who gave birth to her, and because she didn't put her adoptive parents name on the form, we are prevented from reconnecting.

At some point in the midst of my turmoil, I picked up Leonard Nimoy's book, *You and I*, in which he wrote: "I am not immortal. Whatever I put off for later may never be. Whoever doesn't know now that I love them may never know."

This was just how I was feeling. I needed to tell Liddie I loved her now! Each minute that past intensified that need.

* * * * * * * *

Back on my birth mothers' list, I read an e-mail from a woman who felt everyone would be better off if we acknowledged the choice we made by giving our children for adoption. We needed to forgive ourselves and get on with our lives.

The responses from the birth mothers in closed record adoptions were angry ones. "Choice means options. We were given none."

The heated discussion brought me to a new level of understanding of the degree to which I had been traumatized. From the moment I was raped, everything seemed out of my control. Knowing I had no choices because of the dictates of society, I allowed my life to be led by others, following numbly whatever anyone said to do.

Then suddenly, though I continued to think about Liddie, I felt nothing. A wall slid down, isolating me from the world and myself.

Even with new information about how to get Liddie's number, I did nothing. My friend Eva suggested that, since I knew Liddie was a journalist, I should get the names of all the newspapers, look each one up on the Internet and check to see if one employs her. With that, I could get her last name and contact her directly. Great idea, but I had no desire to pursue it and no idea what had come over me. This pain was far worse than any I experienced searching. Why was I putting myself through it?

* * * * * * * *

"You are entitled to your feelings, you know," my therapist said, reassuring me. I had been explaining to her how I hated feeling out of control by my anger. She suggested I write about it.

"The ulcers in my mouth are making it painful to talk. I'm scared too," I said. "I'm just sure if I bring up my anger it will scar my throat and cause me to lose my voice."

My therapist's eyebrows raised at that comment. What I had just said was significant.

But, day after day I thought about my anger and did nothing about it. Finally, realizing nothing was going to hurt as much as my ulcers, I began typing. Slowly, one word came at a time, then more. Finally finished, I was shocked at the extent of my anger, the source was far greater than just losing my daughter.

But, after printing out what I had written, I was surprised at how dull and void of feeling the words looked on paper. In order to heal, I knew I had to read my words out loud and have them heard by those who would understand. My support group seemed like the safest place.

From my seat in the circle, the paper shaking in my trembling hands, I read to the group:

"My rage feels like hot red lava fanning itself throughout my entire body, putting me off balance. The spiral thing again, I guess! I want to hit out, strike back, but don't know who should be the target. I know my anger is coming from someplace deep inside, but for the life of me, I am utterly confused as to how to get rid of it. Where should I place this anger, besides the courts, which in reality are only doing their job?

"I guess my anger started with my abandonment. For all these years, I have felt nothing but sorrow at never having met my birth mother, ignoring the anger I felt at being shoved away from her warm womb into the world of unknown.

"To place my anger in that situation, it has to be with the birth father, as with everything the psychics have said, it was his decision to get rid of me. My modis operandi always rationalized this act away, but today I must own the feeling. My birth father's fear that the church would find out about me, most assuredly caused my mother to go along with his wishes.

"I am also angry that my birth mother, representing all women, allowed herself to be controlled by a man. I have great control issues, maybe that is why. I hate being told what I can and cannot do. I want options so I can make my own decisions."

Beginning to cry now, I went on. "I hate the fact that I was put in semi-isolation in the hospital for six weeks after being found, shunned from the other children. I was isolated like soiled goods, different, possibly defective, not the same. This makes me angry!

"I am angry that my adoptive mother went to the people's house who found me to ask the mother of the house what she thought of me. Heavens, this woman only saw me for a few minutes! I bet she had a feeling I might have come from this family so wanted to observe their surroundings. What she hoped to learn I have no idea, but then again, I came from Mars, so you never know.

"I am angry that I was adopted, angry that I was not like everyone else I knew growing up. I never knew any other adopted children. I am angry not knowing my real birthday. I am angry my life changed after learning I was not their biological child. I am angry my adoptive mother never understood me. I am angry she abused me emotionally and physically. I am angry she did not own up to her feelings concerning her illegitimate father because, if she had, maybe she would not have taken those feelings out on me."

Now my angry feelings intensified. "I am angry that I do not know who looks like me, acts like me, or who mirrors me. I am angry that I have always felt out of place during family reunions. I am angry for always having to try to act a certain way so as not to bring shame to the family. I am angry my free spirit was crushed for acting normal; I am angry that in trying so hard to act the way they wanted me to be, I let my inner self be harmed, preventing my emotional growth. I am angry I never learned to rely on myself, feeling I was not capable of such things.

"I am angry at myself for never having learned about boundaries. I am angry I never knew, until much later in life, that I did in fact have power over my own life.

"I am angry that the church ruled society in 1959. I am angry societal values convinced me that a two-parent family was much better for my child than being with me, while never giving me a choice in the matter. I am angry no one told me what the emotional impact of growing up without your own biological mother could do to you."

Now my stomach was cramping up. "I am angry I rationalized giving Liddie away by saying to myself, 'I was given away, now she is given away.' Like that made it right or something? To even have those thoughts makes me crazy.

"I am angry at the role religion played in my life. First I was Catholic, if the story is true that my birth father was a priest. Then I was adopted into a very religious Lutheran family. I believed in this denomination, but as I look back, there were tell tale signs of unrest. During confirmation lessons, I asked specific questions. After receiving such ambiguous answers of, 'You have to believe, to have faith,' I rebelled. I am angry I had to endure all the letters and pictures of Jesus on the cross my mother sent letting me know I was going to die in Hell for marrying my husband.

"I am angry my mother-in-law took my babies away from me to have them circumcised for their Bris. While I knew it was tradition and it would have hurt me to have seen my little one being cut, the feeling of abandonment was so very real. To this day, I can remember my son Kiley being taken away with all the relatives to the hospital for the ceremony. Left home alone with my nurse, I parted the bedroom curtains and watched them drive away. I did not want my baby to experience being away from me. I cried deep primal tears, shocking the nurse taking care of me."

The room remained quiet as I continued reading. "I am angry at people who profess to being overly religious. My mother was religious, yet chose to beat me, to look down on my type of friends and not accept the fact that God loves everyone, red and yellow, black and white. Not just those she thought acceptable.

"I am angry there are babies still being abandoned by their parents, most likely out of fear because of their religious beliefs, when today there are choices. I am angry that little children are being sexually and emotionally abused and neglected. I am also angry that fathers do not pay child support, but mostly I am angry knowing parents are adopting healthy white children for thousands and thousands of dollars to fulfill their maternal needs. Adoption has become a big business. This causes me great pain.

"I get angry when I realize someone of importance, of power, is putting road blocks in my path. Here I have a daughter wanting to meet me and again a man, this time a judge, is preventing it from happening."

Pausing, I said, "I guess my anger goes back to the beginning of my life, when my birth father made the decision not to keep me."

Emotionally spent, I crumbled in my seat, grateful those around me completely understood.

* * * * * * * *

The next morning, my anger lingered and I wondered how I would ever be purged of it. Hoping to relax my tense muscles, I immersed myself in the hot water from my shower, allowing the water to somehow release me. Had Liddie become fed up with the whole process and tossed the paperwork into her trash?

It had been a few weeks since I heard from Peg. Fearing bad news, I dialed. But, Peg said her form had been returned and entered into the court system a week before. Didn't she understand how important it was to tell me these things?

Meanwhile, I still had my Internet friends helping with the search. My connection in Amsterdam, Chris, e-mailed me to let me know that he had not been able to track a birth record for Liddie's second child, born January 8, 1996. None of the babies born that date had an English sounding name.

Then, on March 15, 1996, the call I had been waiting so long for finally came. It was seven in the evening. I remember making note of it as I answered the phone.

Peg's voice sounded elated. "I have wonderful news for you. It's a go! I can now give you your daughter's name. Without a pause in which I could have caught my breath, she said, "Her name is Ludia Margaret Austin, and here is her address!"

Could I actually believe what I was hearing? All my hard work, pain and anguish were finally coming to an end. I felt a sudden urge to have pink bubble gum cigars to pass out to everyone!

* * * * * * * *

Finally having Liddie's name and address, I sat down to my computer to write her. But, still no words would come. Suddenly, the task seemed overwhelming, especially with my friend Eva's comments stuck in my mind. I would be writing a stranger, she had said. Yet, I felt I had known my daughter all of her life. Perhaps seeing her letter to me would unblock something.

When Liddie's letter arrived from Peg, I stared at the unfamiliar handwriting on the envelope. I couldn't get over how nicely she wrote. I kissed the envelope and held it close to my heart for the longest while before opening it. I had waited so long for this letter.

Finding a quiet place in the house where I could spend time alone with my daughter, I carefully opened the letter and began reading it, savoring every word. At the very end of the letter, Liddie wrote, "I look forward to hearing more from and about you." How I treasured those words.

My emotions were mixed as I lay the letter aside. I felt happy, sad, elated, and depressed. Nothing was ever going to make up for the time we had lost with each other. Now, we were two adoptees, mother and daughter, about to start our journey. At that moment, it was hard to see that this was actually the second leg of the journey we had always been on together.

My letter in my head I wanted to send her grew to such a size that the pages would have carpeted the floor of a large room. Realizing this would be way too overwhelming, I wrote and wrote until I had a letter of manageable length.

Then I copied my letter from my computer onto beautiful handmade paper I had purchased just for this occasion. After slipping in pictures of myself, and the boys, I headed for the post office to have it weighed.

"Is this your daughter?" the post lady asked. "Then you may want a sheet showing foreign rates, if you will be sending things there often."

As if it were the most natural thing, I said, "Yes, this is my daughter." Leaving the post office, I literally skipped to the car. That post lady had no idea how wonderful she had made me feel!

Now, with the letter mailed. All I could do was wait for her reply. In the meantime, everything seemed to go into slow motion. Unable to focus on anything, I slept a lot. Nothing was getting done around the house. The refrigerator was bare and I didn't even care. It was almost as if I had mailed myself to Amsterdam along with my letter.

I stopped going to my therapist and began missing appointments. My checkbook would not balance because I kept forgetting to write down the checks I had written. With all my energy focused practically on the other side of the world, I felt depleted. Sleep became impossible.

Since I was being so unproductive, I decided to make Liddie a scrapbook, something I could give her when we met. With no specific design in mind, I just let my intuition take over and guide the creation of it.

First, I found a 1959 Life Magazine published the day before she was born. Then I discovered the cover from a 1933 American Home Magazine that would make the perfect cover for the scrapbook. It had hearts and lace and old-fashioned cards. Inside, I put postcards showing the area where I lived when I was pregnant with her, and added a few of my favorite children's verses, along with pictures of myself growing up and my adoptive family. It was so much fun putting it together. Still, much of the material began to gather dust as I often lacked the energy to work on it.

* * * * * * * *

A new level of awareness had come with this new connection with my daughter and, therefore, inevitable reproaching questions. How could I have been coerced into surrendering my child? Why didn't I challenge the system? Why did I stay behind those closed hospital room doors like I was told to? Why didn't I sneak a peak into the nursery to see my own child? What great force kept me from doing the most natural thing in the world? Why did I sign those papers? I had always been a rebel about everything else in my life.

Again, I went to the library. I could always find answers there. First, I went to the travel section to find a book on Amsterdam. But, instead of finding a book on Holland, I discovered one that must have been accidentally placed on the wrong shelf - *The Fifties - The Way We Really Were.* Or had an angel placed it there? I raced home to begin reading it.

My teenage years spanned this decade, but as I read I realized I had not been very conscious during that time in my life. According to the authors, while overall the fifties were a "time of conformity and status, anxiety, sexual repressions and political apathy of the young," this historical period had three distinct phases.

The first phase, from 1948-1953, what the authors called the "Age of Fear," I would have been nine through fourteen years of age. While I could not remember President Truman announcing plans to develop a hydrogen bomb, I did remember about Senator Joseph McCarthy and his anti-communist witch hunt. If one were to believe the senator, communists were everywhere.

In schools, during recess, children were offered, free from the government, peanut butter and crackers, cheese and pint size containers of milk always served warm. Everyone was encouraged to buy war bonds or enter art poster contests showing their love of America. During this time, I remember discovering I hated sports, loved books (either the Bobsy Twins series or biographies), and often stood strong on principle, which usually got me into trouble.

At that age, I was responsible for helping with chores around the house. Dusting seemed an exercise in futility, since the coal dust from the furnace would cover the furniture almost as soon as I finished dusting. At times, when someone would forget to stoke the furnace, a putrid smell would fill the house, causing everyone to rush outside for clean air to breathe.

There would be the yearly individual pictures taken at the Olan Mills Studio, located over Woolworth's five and ten cent store, which were then slipped into the already hanging 8 x 10 wooden shadowbox frames, instantly creating an updated family. Girl Scout activities, piano lessons, the church choir and active involvement in church activities occupied my time.

The second era, from 1954-1957, the authors called "The Era of Conservative Consensus." This encompassed the years fifteen through eighteen for me. My recollection of the downfall of Senator McCarthy and the Life Magazine photo of the death of Stalin were vivid. During this period, the authors said, "Young people overwhelmingly accepted the value of their elders and dedicated themselves to the bourgeois goals of security, sociability and domesticity. They went steady, married young, had lots of children, lived the conforming life of 'togetherness.'"

My expression of togetherness was meeting all my friends at the Palace, a confectionery store, after school. In the front of the store, display cases showed beautiful handmade chocolates lovingly arranged on paper doilies. Handmade suckers, cellophane wrapped, stuck out of jars, revealing their unique shapes. One jar held rock candy. A Greek family owned the store, my first experience with someone foreign, and I liked it.

Across from the display case was the soda fountain bar. Slipping onto one of the red vinyl covered chrome stools facing the mirror-backed fountain to order a cherry or lemon coke, or maybe a short chocolate (chocolate milk with ice), the reflected view of the candy display continued to tempt.

But it was in the back of the store where all the action happened. Immediately after school, teenagers rushed to the Palace to meet their friends. Rushing by the candy display to get a seat, they filled the booths in the back. A colorful jukebox separated the front of the store from the back. Everyone ordered the same thing, cokes and bags of chips, and socialized before they were expected home to do their homework. We were blissfully unaware at least consciously that, according to the authors, "58% of the populace questioned favored finding all communists even if some innocent people should get hurt, and that 78% thought it a good idea to report to the FBI, neighbors or acquaintances whom they suspected of being communists, especially if they appeared at all strange or different."

But, I did not escape the oppressive conservatism, especially on Sundays which were always the same. Everyone I knew attended Sunday school and church. No establishments were open because of Pennsylvania's Blue Laws. I was never certain what that term meant, but I knew they were the cause of all the stores being closed, leaving teenagers with nothing to do. Watching the Ed Sullivan Show was the highlight of the day.

Toward the end of the fifties, the authors felt, "Crisis still existed because poverty, racism, sexism and militarism were threatening America." They felt, "The people were a society made up of a generation who could not believe society would let them down. They were suburbanized, bureaucratized, smug and secure."

The fact that the blacks had to live on the other side of the railroad tracks was something I had been very aware of. The saying, "Oh, she lives on the other side of the railroad tracks," had nothing to do with location. It was a derogatory remark when applied to anyone, black or white.

Segregation of the blacks and the poor had puzzled me, especially after visiting the home of my black friend Jackie. Just walking into her home made me feel like I was breaking a law, which felt very good actually. My eyes widened when I saw the big grand piano in the living room, something I would have expected to find only in the most expensive houses in town. If Jackie's family could afford a piano of such grandeur, why couldn't they live on the other side of the tracks? It was in Jackie's house that I first heard Rhythm and Blues music, later called Rock and Roll.

"Life started to change when Rock and Roll became popular, contributing to a new era." According to the authors, "The Rock and Rollers were leaving an American culture day dreaming of a false world with Mr. Clean, Doris Day, General Ike and universal luxury, without stress, Negroes or genitalia. Rock was one of the forces that woke us up."

These latter years were the ones during which I was getting ready to graduate from high school. Drugs were never a problem in our school. It was alcohol that caused problems. On our senior outing, some classmates were ejected from the bus for using a hypodermic needle to shoot vodka into oranges and watermelons to create a spiked fruit cocktail. A definite no-no.

The years from 1959 to 1960 were called by the authors, "The Time of National Reassessment." During those years, I was between eighteen and twenty-one, struggling with college and my repressed adoption issues, then studying to fly with the airlines.

During the fifties, the best selling book was the *Revised Standard Version of the Bible*. My mother thought the fact that people were tampering with the Bible was a sure sign society was going to hell.

The author's felt the reason people turned to religion in record numbers was "to find hope in an anxious world brought on by the hydrogen bombs. Atomic spies made the churches seem the mainstay of traditional values." Names like Norman Vincent Peale and Bishop Fulton Sheen had popular television shows and radio programs. Their popularity could be compared to the rock stars of today.

Both *A Man Named Peter* and *The Power of Positive Thinking* were prominently displayed at our house, while heated discussions continued concerning the *Revised Standard Version of the Bible.*

Curled up on the couch, I was most eager to read the author's take on sex and relationships in the fifties. Would I find a clue as to why I gave my daughter away?

"Sex roles," the authors wrote, "always had to be maintained in the fifties. Males were the aggressive partners, females the passive ones. She had to be a 'good girl,' a virgin on the wedding night. An unsatisfying sexual relationship, most emphatically, was the fault of the woman. Then sexual repression was remodeled. A wife could enjoy sex as long as she obediently catered to her man."

There it was. If you weren't a virgin on your wedding night, you were considered a slut, no matter how the sexual relationship came about. Even in the case of rape. This was why I felt so responsible.

Norman Mailer's blunt description of the fifties as, "one of the worst decades in the history of man," was one I would have to agree with.

*　　*　　*　　*　　*　　*　　*　　*

Three weeks had passed since I sent my letter to Liddie and I was getting anxious. Finally, I just couldn't run hopefully to the mailbox every day and then flip the lid closed in disappointment. So, I stopped checking the mail altogether. Of course, everyone was asking if I'd heard anything. I felt just like I did when I was overdue with my sons and everyone was asking, "Are you still here?"

But then, one day, when I was absentmindedly flipping through the stacks of bills, letters and catalogs, I found myself staring at an envelope carrying three Dutch stamps. Recognizing the now familiar handwriting, I went in search of a quiet spot to read it.

As I pulled the letter from the envelope, something floated onto my lap. When I looked to see what it was, an electric shock passed through my body. I was looking into a mirror. It was a picture of Liddie and she looked just like me. Holding her picture to my heart, I realized I was seeing for the first time the only female who was directly and genetically related to me. Liddie was proof of a lineage so unfamiliar to me.

Another picture was stuck in among the pages. It was of Liddie's immediate family, all seated together on their couch. On the back of the photo were all their names: Arjan, her boyfriend and father of her two girls; Jet, her oldest daughter, now two and a half; and, Cato only three weeks old. Seeing my granddaughters for the first time brought me pure joy. Completely in love, I wanted to shout my ecstasy to the rooftops!

The third picture was the hardest to look at. It was a picture of Liddie as a baby. Ink from her letter had rubbed off onto the photograph, causing ink marks to mar the baby's face. Surprisingly, I felt nothing. The baby could have been anyone.

Hoping to discover some resemblance to myself as a baby, I searched through my personal pictures. But, sadly, I could find no pictures of myself at the same age. The little outfit she wore, caused me a twinge of jealousy that another mother had dressed her. The strangeness of her surroundings struck me. Forced to imagine Liddie with others, I put the picture away and promptly lost it somewhere in the house.

My heart broke when Liddie said she wondered who at the 'children's' home' saw her first smile. Surely her adoptive mother saw her first smile. Liddie had only been in the foster home a few weeks. This must have been her way of describing her feelings of abandonment.

From her letter, I was learning just how much alike we were. We both had bad feet and allergies. Liddie liked to cook, read, write and shop - all the things I enjoyed.

My response to her letter grew long again. In my first letter to her, I told Liddie to please ask any questions and I promised to tell the truth. She took my offer seriously and by the time I answered all her questions, the letter ended up nine pages long. It was not the short letter everyone had advised me to write. But, Liddie deserved answers.

The only question I struggled with was about her birth father. This was a question I wanted to answer in person. Telling her about the rape in a letter didn't seem right. But,

I told her his name and what I had learned from the adoption agency a few months before, that he was Scotch/Irish and twenty-eight years old when I was pregnant with her. I did say he abandoned me when he learned of my pregnancy, and that he probably still lived in Detroit, Michigan.

When I finished the letter, life felt so wonderful. Nothing seemed impossible. The next day, I rushed to the mall to have Kodak copies made of her pictures so I could send them to family and friends. While there, I had them blow up Liddie's family picture to an 8 x 10 size and slipped it into a frame I found on the store shelf. In addition, I made a copy of Liddie's headshot and framed it, too, so each day I could carry it from my nightstand to my computer and back.

Wanting to share my joy with the world, I sat for days addressing envelopes that contained the announcement of my reunion with my daughter. As my joy increased each day, so did the number of announcements I sent out. Even the Judge in Michigan who was assigned to my case received one with a little side note that said, "This was what searching was all about."

Letters and phone calls began pouring in from everyone. My cousin Gretchen sent me a 'Congratulations On Your New Baby Girl' card, with the word 'baby' crossed out. The card was all pink, which was even more meaningful since I had raised three boys. My friend Eva sent flowers, which felt like Liddie's birth was now properly legitimized.

In a loving card, my sister said she cried when she saw Liddie's pictures because of the strong resemblance. She felt Liddie and I had the same hands, and when I took a closer look I thought she might be right.

For the next three weeks, the joy and adrenalin coursing through me relieved all my aches and pains. Even my stomach stopped hurting. If I could just bottle this euphoria!

CHAPTER ELEVEN

Again, I was anxiously awaiting a reply from Liddie. And Mother's Day was fast approaching. Always before, I looked forward to the celebration. But, this year it was creating an uneasy feeling. Did they celebrate Mother's Day in Holland? Would Liddie think of me? How would I feel if I found my own mother? Though I tried to put myself in Liddie's shoes, my adopted side could not give my birth mother side answers.

When my youngest son, Daniel, received Liddie's pictures in the announcement, he was not prepared for the funny feeling in the pit of his stomach. "She looks just like you," he said. "This makes everything different. If she had looked like someone else, then I don't think I would have these feelings. But now, Wow!"

Finally, after a year and a half, the barrier of silence hovering over my search and reunion, was broken. Soon after receiving Daniel's response, Jay, startled me with his. Walking into the house, he went straight to the tape recorder and popped in a tape. "I wrote this song for you," he announced. "Come and listen."

The song was titled, "Who Am I?" and was performed by his garage band.

Verse I

I just got some bad news today
It seems my parents gave me away
They left me on a stranger's porch and ran away
There I was all alone, cold and hungry, just two weeks
old

Not even knowing what would become of my destiny
What did I do to you, why don't you want me?
Was I a bad child or was I just fat and ugly?
I'm an innocent child, so scared and all alone

(Hey hope there's someone home)

Verse II

After what seemed like a while, someone opened the door
They said, "Hey look Ma, here's a child for us to love
We'll bring it in from the cold, we'll give it a
name and give it some clothes
We'll send her to school and she'll swim in our pool
We're gonna make her one of us
We're gonna teach her to smile, hang at the mall for awhile
She's gonna be the best damn kid that you have ever seen
Yet, with all these glories, there's one thing still troubling me

(Hey, does anybody know me?)

Guitar solo

Verse III

Now I'm trying to find myself, I don't know where to start
I've read all the books, done all the work, yet it still seems so dark,
I don't know what I'm looking for, except for some piece of mind
To know who I am, to know where I'm from
Will I feel like this all the time?
I feel so empty, with no one by my side

The hardest thing for me, is I've been searching for all my life
Yet, I'm not any closer to who I could possibly be
Hey, does anybody know me, I said
Hey, does anybody care, I said
Hey, does anybody love me, I said
Hey, does anybody care ....?

Listening to my son's song, all the pain I had been experiencing during the search was brought to the surface. My children were hurting for me. Was this a sign for me to get back to the search for my birth parents? I desperately needed closure.

* * * * * * * *

With closure as a goal, I wrote to my Internet friend from Maryland to let him know I was returning to the search for my birth parents and needed direction. Richard wrote back suggesting that when I return to the east coast I should check death records and obituaries. "Your birth mother would be in her seventies," he wrote. "And if what the psychics have said is true, that your father is much older than your mother, he would probably be deceased."

His e-mail went on to say, "You should look for clues in the obituaries. Look at the one for the man who's house you were placed, the detectives who investigated your case, perhaps the ministers and priests of the area churches. Thomasville was the chosen place, not just a convenient place, so there is a connection or a reason why you were left there. The obituary might mention where someone went to school, served in the military, where they came from or went. If your birth father was a priest, perhaps he had a family in Thomasville, or maybe he had a contact (another priest) in the area who could keep him informed or advised him of your placement. Look in old town directories, church records, old newspapers."

He emphasized, "You must be ready for such a journey and cannot enter the past with obligations and worries tying you to the present. Perhaps you can resume your search when resolutions to your questions have come to you by way of your daughter, and when you have released the answers to her questions." Now that I read his letter, I wondered if I should put this search aside for now.

* * * * * * * *

Another letter arrived from my daughter, this time eighteen pages. And it was written on Mother's Day!

From her letter, I learned that Liddie spoke Russian and had traveled all over Europe, Russia and the United States, doing interviews for her women's magazine. She stopped her travels when her first daughter was born. Her family was considering moving back to the United States, to Mission Viejo, California, which shocked me because that was just a few miles from where I was now living. But Liddie wasn't happy with the prospect. "I did not want to move to Holland as a child but now feeling at home in Holland, I did not want to move again," she wrote. To think we could have been neighbors!

Her response to my request about what gifts the children might enjoy from me was books in English for Jet so she could learn the language. Learning that Liddie was still an American citizen made my heart soar. Her citizenship status was proof of our continual link.

Liddie made me laugh when she said the reason she never searched for me was because she was afraid I might have been "ugly or a murderer or both." She said, "I feel comfortable telling you this now since I know this isn't the case." She also felt it was "better to be safe than sorry; better to have nice thoughts about someone out there than to search (always the mother; the father never really interested me)."

Twirling around and around the room, hugging her letter to my heart, I was thrilled to realize we were starting a relationship.

Almost immediately, I became consumed with finding the perfect gift to give Liddie when we met. Several of my birth mother friends suggested something they had given, a gold bracelet as that would symbolize a circle that was now complete. But, somehow, when I found the perfect gold bracelet, it didn't feel personal enough to me. After discussing my problem with Ross, he said he would design something for Liddie.

He drew a small medallion, smaller than a quarter but larger than a dime, with our Hebrew initials in the middle. It would be cut out of a gold circle, to hang from a gold chain. No one would know what it meant. I loved the idea and called our custom jeweler to have it made up.

In the Jewish faith, an infant girl is brought to the altar by her parents and named in front of God. Since Liddie had been born before I converted, I was not certain whether I could use a Hebrew name for her, or Hebrew letters for that matter. Wanting the gift to be just right, I called my friend, Cantor Wetzler in Lansing, Michigan, and in a roundabout way asked him if the name Liddie in Hebrew would carry the letter 'L,' as I was making an initial necklace. This man who had converted me to Judaism, taught all my sons Hebrew for their Bar Mitzvahs, supported me during my two year term as sisterhood president, confirmed two of my sons in Michigan, flew to California to officiate at my youngest son's Bar Mitzvah and led the choir in which I was a member, was never told about my daughter. It was time he knew.

After finding the strength to tell him about her, the Cantor suggested in an even voice, "Let's find a name for your daughter." Researching through his book, he exclaimed, "Here is her name. Her Hebrew name is Lebah (meaning my love), middle name Miriam (the sister of

Moses who was an adoptee), bat Sarah (your Hebrew first name.)"

My naming her in this way was not a problem, he said. "Even though you converted to Judaism after she was born, because of the circumstances of your pregnancy, since it was not your fault, she can be named and she is Jewish. You are to forget the father's last name. Because of what he did to you, he does not deserve to have his name attached to hers, and that is why I am using your first name as her last."

The Cantor then pronounced, "This is your daughter," just as if we were in temple.

After thanking him and hanging up the phone, I just sobbed. He had just named my daughter, and validated her birth in the eyes of God. Even though I wasn't certain how Liddie would feel about having a Jewish name, for me I could now say thirty-six years later, "My daughter, Lebah Miriam Sarah, now has a legitimate name, a name blessed by God."

* * * * * * * *

My back ached. Glancing at the clock I realized I had been working on Liddie's scrap book for eight straight hours, almost as if I were possessed.

Wanting to add some poetry I had enjoyed as a child, I dug around my bookcase and found an old booklet titled, "Poems for Elementary Age School Children" that was not familiar to me. It must have come from my late mother's estate.

Leafing through the book to see if there were poems I could remember, out fell two small squares of yellow construction paper with poems on them. One poem was about using a hankie to cover your mouth when having a cold so you don't spread germs, and the other was about brushing your teeth. It was eerie seeing my mother's handwriting so many years after her death.

Dangling gingerly from the back of the booklet was another poem. At first, all I could read was its title, "Where's Mother?"

When I was a child from one to four,
I played near Mother on the floor,
But when she left the sitting room
To draw the tea or get the broom,
I cried, "Where's Mother?"

When I was old enough to play,
In the big front yard or the new mown hay,
I'd call aloud as before,
"Where's Mother?"

Then, having grown beyond my teens,
I wandered away to other scenes,
Often my footsteps were retraced
And I was back at the Old Home place,
Calling, "Where's Mother?'

Finally, I left home for a larger life,
And entered a field of struggle and strife.
But often returned, as in days of yore,
To meet my mother at the old front door,
And cry, "Where's Mother?"

One day I returned and Mother slept,
With a peaceful smile, but I turned and wept,
Since then I return to the same old farm,
But to me it has lost its greatest charm,
For my heart yearns to say,
"Where's Mother?"

Teardrops stained Liddie's book by the time I finished reading the poem. Birth mother, adoptive mother, Liddie's mother, natural mother and grandmother - too many mothers to think about. Everything felt jumbled up inside: mothers, sadness, loss. My adoptee feelings entwined with my birth mother feelings creating chaos. A visit to the therapist seemed necessary.

With confidence, Dr. Mantecon pronounced I was grieving for my adoptive mother. Affirming her opinion, I told her I hadn't really had time to cry at her funeral. "I was too busy taking care of details my mother was requesting," I explained. "Her spirit spoke in my ear at the viewing and said I should make sure everyone was taken care of, to be a good hostess. So I did my best."

"Your psyche knows when it is time for you to do your mourning," Dr. Mantecon assured me. "Finding the poems triggered points of pain that needed to be dealt with, and your psyche felt you could handle it now."

Grieving for my adoptive mother was still difficult given I still felt like I never measured up.

"Everyone has something, even if only one speck of goodness that can be mourned," she replied. "You have to separate both feelings, to honor the pain and to honor the good parts. You know, since you gave Liddie the gift of knowing you, this makes the void of not knowing your own natural mother even greater. You are also grieving the inability of your adoptive mother to have mothered you in the way you so desperately needed. Feel your pain and cry your tears. It is a healing."

But I had to wonder if I were in the birth mother mode or the adoptee mode in my mourning. "You are in the adoptee mode," she said.

As we broached the subject of my rape, I realized I must not be finished with the subject since my feelings were still raw. "I still feel guilty about it," I confessed. "Maybe it was my fault. My daddy had told me there was no such thing as rape. I can even remember him using the analogy of trying to thread a moving needle. He actually took white thread and, with his elbows on the table, moved the needle back and forth while trying to stick the thread through the hole. 'See,' he had said. 'It can't be done!' And then he added that women can run faster with their skirts up than men can with their pants down."

"Society sets women up to be raped by having this silent understanding that men should be aggressive and women passive," Dr. Mantecon replied. "You gave him body language which said, 'No.' You were raped and it was not your fault. Guilt comes from society and gets in the way of your feelings, which are always valid."

Rehashing events of that evening, I realized after he forced himself on me, he never called again. "He used me!" I said. "He probably thought all airline stewardesses were easy."

* * * * * * * *

In my next letter to Liddie, I found myself writing as if we had known each other forever. We could now write about our daily lives after catching up on lifetimes. I told her about our family weekend to celebrate Daniel's graduation from college, and how proud we were of him. I felt comfortable sharing an article by an adoptive mother and Ph.D. that I found in my "Roots and Wings" publication.

The author, Dr. Barbara Tremetiere, realizing just how important genetics were in the adoptive family wrote, "Many adoptive parents want the child they adopted to come with a clean slate; to become just like them. When that does not happen, they feel they have failed. They wonder why it often seemed that the relationship with their child felt out of sync."

The author also believed that, "The responsibility of any parent is to support their children's talents, abilities, thoughts, dreams and goals, to help them become their unique self." When the author searched for and found the birth parents for her children, she said, "It explained so much. They were like their birth parents."

I was explaining myself to Liddie as much as I was offering her information. "Reading the article made me understand why I always felt out of sync with my adoptive family," I wrote. "And how they never seemed to understand me. I feel connected genetically to you, Liddie, and environmentally connected to my parents. I am so glad your parents helped you reach your dreams and goals." I included a poem by an on-line friend entitled "Family Tree."

Rereading the article on genetics before sending it, I was amazed to discover that the author was an adoption specialist for the Tressler Lutheran Services in York, Pennsylvania, the town next to the village where I was left. Every Thursday, my dad would fix the orphan's teeth there for free, and sometimes, still too young to go to school, I went with him. It was only dawning on me at that moment that very well might have been my home, too.

With my missal off to Liddie, I returned to the waiting mode, hoping for a quick reply. When it came, I was surprised to find how down she was in the letter, since it was so different from the last happy one. "The children will call you Sally," she wrote. "As my parents would be very hurt if they heard the children talking about another 'Oma'."

My stomach twinged as I took in this development. Those children were of my blood. Children don't have preconceived notions about all this. I could simply be another Oma. Damn! I hated all this.

Liddie went on to say that she had never really had any adoption issues.

"I do not need to know where I am from to know where I am going, because I know where I am going. I have never felt the need to know my roots."

It seemed clear that Liddie did not really need me, at least not as much and in the way I needed her. Writing of her findings in adoption research was probably a mistake. What was I doing butting into her life? Here I thought I was giving her a gift, but now I believed she was just being polite in accepting it, when in reality she would just as soon send the gift back. Damn! I let my guard down. Why didn't I just write a friendly letter instead of the mother-daughter letter I sent.

Responding to one of my questions concerning her mother's ability to survive the war as a German Jew during the Nazi regime, Liddie wrote, "My mother and her family moved from Germany to Holland at age three. Because the grandmothers on both sides had a child out of wedlock and refused to say who the fathers were, tracing their lineage was impossible, so they were spared. The rest of their family did die during that time leaving the family small."

Concerning her religious affiliations, Liddie said, "When we were small, all the children in our family were baptized Lutheran so in case there is another war, we would not be Jewish." She added that she was also not religious. Our religious lives were flip flopped.

*   *   *   *   *   *   *   *

Finally, I just felt a great need to meet my daughter. So Ross and I decided to spend our wedding anniversary, August 11, in Amsterdam. Where else? We had enough frequent flier miles for the trip as it turned out, which elated both of us. But, then we learned the amount of miles needed doubled during high season, and procuring regular tickets proved difficult during high season for international travel.

Reserving our seats through a travel agent, we found the tickets were nonrefundable. The thought of losing thousands of dollars, if we had to cancel the trip because it was not a good time for Liddie, was enough to erase any fears of calling her before finalizing our tickets.

With heightened anticipation, knowing I would be hearing my daughter's voice for the first time, I dialed her number. It was not a good call.

* * * * * * * *

In all the birth mother books I had ever read, the authors talked about how wonderful it was to finally hear their child's voice after so many lost years. This call did not feel wonderful to me at all. Unfamiliar emotions arose within me as I realized I had just scared my daughter to death. Never in my life had I ever made anyone feel so uncomfortable. Even though the call lasted only long enough to tell Liddie of our travel plans and to apologize for the last letter, it seemed to go on forever.

After hanging up, I wondered what I could have done wrong? First I wrote her a letter that made her sad. And then I called her and scared her out of her wits. Now it is my turn to write and I am afraid to say anything. One thing was for certain, I would not be writing about adoption issues. Perhaps I shouldn't even talk about the boys.

A few days later, I received an email from a psychologist friend advising me to wait to give Liddie the necklace. The gesture might be too much for her, and I should wait until we know each other better. Suddenly, I found myself slipping into my now familiar deep black hole. It felt like I couldn't do anything right. The multitude of pieces to this complex puzzle were not taking shape. Each time I tried to add a new piece, it just didn't fit. Perhaps it would be best not to go to Amsterdam.

Over lunch, my friend Adelyn suggested I might be trying to force the pieces to fit into my puzzle. One day the puzzle would come together. I just needed to be patient. It was going to take time.

But, driving home I had a revelation. Talking to Liddie had upset me so much because, when I heard this grown woman's foreign accent on the phone, I realized my child was no longer my baby. I had lost my baby for the second time.

Despite finding her, there was still a hole deep inside that was screaming to be filled, the need just as strong as an addict's craving begging a fix. How would I ever silence it? In the strangest way, it was like my umbilical cord remembered being severed and needed to be hooked back up for my throbbing pain to finally stop.

The feeling built that I was about to go over the edge. The pain in my stomach now caused me to double up. I could not sleep, and when I managed to, I slept too much. By now I knew what I had to do was purge my feelings.

Engulfed in my loss, with tears flowing like an unplugged dike, I grabbed for the stationery and wrote without pausing:

> Dear Liddie,
>
> All my friends are telling me I am trying too hard in this relationship. While I know this to be true, I don't know what to do about it, since I love you so much. I do not want to invade your personal boundaries and want our reunion to be wonderful. Maybe we need a password to use when I visit in case I come on too strong? Birth mother would be a good one. Whenever I hear it, I will know to back off. I just don't want you to feel uncomfortable.

Not even waiting to proof the letter, I pushed it through the mailbox slot before changing my mind.

* * * * * * * *

The next morning, while lying in bed, I wondered how another human being could have such an effect on me. After all, Liddie was made like me: skin, bones, blood, water and a dent in our noses. How could this stranger, though my daughter, this stranger with a Dutch accent and living in a totally different culture, make me feel like every nerve in my body was being played.

Was it Liddie who was playing my nerves, or was it my own fears of rejection? She may not even like me. This line of thought I swore I would never go down.

Mentally, physically and emotionally exhausted, I backed off reading birth mother literature, stopped hanging out on the Internet so much, worked around the house, went shopping, and got back to living my life. Helpless to change anything, I remembered my sister's words: "You cannot be responsible for someone else's feelings." I realized it was impossible to put a puzzle together without having the finished picture on the box as a guide. When I met my daughter, all I could do was be myself.

* * * * * * * *

The following week, my granddaughter arrived for her yearly visit and was a great diversion. One day, on our way out the door to make sand castles at the beach, I grabbed the mail and found a troubling letter from Liddie.

For the rest of the week, I read the letter many times, turning her words over and over in my head. Finally, unable to hold my feelings in any longer, I just had to sit down and reconnect with my birth mother support on the Internet.

Subject: Liddie's letter
Date: 96-07-20
From: SJH
To: Birth mother list.com

Dear Ladies,

I wanted to let you know I received a letter from Liddie concerning my trip to Amsterdam. After reading it, I was upset. (Remember I sent her a note telling her I was falling apart emotionally and decided we needed a password?) Well, she was very sweet about that problem. She even searched out a birth mother therapist to help me. Not to help Liddie, but me.

The therapist told her, "The biggest problem in such situations was to find a forum for the relationship which is so unknown (and in a way also unnatural) in this society. Each other is flesh and blood and still complete strangers." Liddie goes on to say that she understands my confusion and that she is also convinced of my good intentions, that this must be so strange for me with my history (being a foundling and adopted).

Then she said, "I have realized from the beginning that you have projected (some of) your own feelings on me and that makes it somewhat difficult for me, because I am not you. But probably my fear of disappointing you originates in this feeling. I wasn't mistaken either. You were a bit disappointed in me. But perhaps it was for the best."

My friends, at this point, I realize I have an intellectualizing daughter, one who does not wish to get in touch with her feelings. I also feel she was somewhat condescending and I am not going to take that from anyone. I reread my letters to her and in no way did I impose my adoption issues on her. I think she already had these issues inside her and did not like the fact that I expressed mine.

Liddie continued her letter by saying my card made her sad. "I admire you very much, being able to see through your own feelings. But, how painful it must be. I think it is very important for both of us to acknowledge the fact, we cannot deny it. Now, thirty-six years later, we have found each other, but we do not know each other.

In a way, we are mother and daughter and if you feel that way towards me, that is O.K., but on another level, we are strangers, who will have to get to know each other and that takes time. I think we should take that time and with an open mind. I think we shall like each other, but who knows? As you well know, even mothers and daughters who have known each other all their lives don't always get along."

Her letter continued with how difficult it was for her to cope with expectations. "If I have the impression that people 'expect' certain feelings from me, I go 'empty.' I do not know what I feel anymore and just want to run. So, the more freedom you let me have, the better."

I felt warmly towards her for honestly sharing her thoughts with me, but then she hit me again when discussing my phone call to her: "Your telephone call took me by surprise. I knew you had my number. I had noticed that on the package you sent. I didn't like that very much - my telephone number was the one boundary I kept and I hoped you would respect that. I understand you had your reasons to call anyway, but still ... I have my needs as well." Then she continued on with caring comments only to hit me again by suggesting, "I seek professional help on these complicated feelings."

She casually mentions she and her boyfriend would be coming to New York City in October (when I will be in Pennsylvania, only a few hours away.) But it was her last statement that made me livid. She said, "What do you want, arriving in Holland? A jet lagged CONFRONTATION or better later in the hotel?"

After reading her letter, I honestly do not want to go to Amsterdam. I know you will all say, things will be better once you meet in person, but I feel I will be meeting an adoptee who has denied her feelings for a very long time. That I will find an intellectual, unemotional person ready to jump on me for giving her up. She, I am sure, is very angry at me if she feels our meeting will be a confrontation. I wrote back to her anyway and said I felt meeting at the hotel better. (Well there goes the airport meeting, like she couldn't wait to meet me thing.)

You will never hear of me calling her again. I have such a problem with phone calls anyway and when I finally got up my nerve to call, she gives me hell for it. I have no idea why that upset her so. I hate this.

I am not comforted knowing I am going to meet a person who has no adoption issues, has a full life, who admires me on one level, but on the other blames me for dumping my adoption issues on her. She wants this confrontation over with and thinks I should get professional counseling after sharing my emotions with her, yet wants us to just be ourselves. I think at the moment I would rather walk on glass.

I have kept this all in for days. I have gone from anger, as I felt she was very condescending, to flitting around the house stating, "No one will put me down. I have done that to myself all my life and By God, she, daughter or not, will not be allowed to do this to me." Then I tried to figure out what I wanted. Maybe that was what is upsetting me? I wanted her to be glad to see me and to let me give her a hug and to let things move from there, like on TV. Hey, it isn't going to happen.

Then I try to remember what you all say, that I should be happy she is alive and that I found her. But I WANT MORE!!!! I know she can never be my daughter, but she will always be my daughter. Then I wonder why I woke up all these emotions I have held in check for 36 years? You will all say, because you needed to work on your issues as they were there anyway. Yeah ... that is right. I did fine, up until I became obsessed. Everyone just loves to be around an obsessed person. Sometimes I make myself sick!

You do your search, your emotional work, and then what? You are left with your obsessed emotional feelings and no contact again? Or, a child who needs to back off emotionally? People say, 'They are busy leading their own lives.' Well, what the hell do you do with your life? Sit back and become a philosopher? Everything will work out the way it is supposed to or statements to make one feel better? Nothing makes it better. Can you tell I am angry?

Sorry this is so long, but I needed to vent. I do not look forward to this trip. I could have jumped into New York City for a few hours, at much less expense, for our confrontation, but she chose not to share this bit of information with me until now.

Talk to you soon.

Sally

By the time I had finished my letter to my friends, I was angry and upset. Still needing to talk my feelings out, Ross and I discussed everything for hours. The next day, I sent another letter to my friends.

Subject: The Amsterdam Trip
Date: 96-07-21
From: SJH
To: Birth mother list.com

Dear Ladies,

After ranting and raving to you last evening, Ross and I sat up until 2:00 AM discussing my feelings. We hashed and rehashed everything that had transpired until now and he agreed with me. My feelings: I was pushing myself on Liddie. She did not ask for any of this. I decided to make this trip. She has never said she looked forward to meeting me, instead wondered where the CONFRONTATION would take place.

So many little things she had said I let pass, chocking it up to the fact that she was scared. I told Ross, "I always take four days to process my thoughts before making major decisions and four days later I am still angry. My decision is being made for me. I will not go to Amsterdam." We discussed going there just for a vacation, but Ross said, "No, you would be crying all the time you are there."

This is how I am going to handle the situation. I will write and tell her I do not feel comfortable flying at this time due to the Trans World Airline bombing. At least that is not a lie. Also, that I never wanted our meeting to be a confrontation. But, maybe we could hook up while she is in New York City for a drink or dinner. Casual, but not a confrontation.

In my pacing and thinking about this relationship, the one thing I know for sure is, I want for her to, some day, actually want to know me. The timing isn't right and I am willing to wait.

It will cost a lot of money to cancel all my plans, but I feel so strongly in my gut that this is the BEST thing to do right now. Liddie has to make the decision in this reunion. She already expressed how she hates expectations, how she needs her freedom. Now she will have it.

Sorry I dumped this all on you last evening, but it helped me make my decision.

Talk to you soon,

Sally

By not going to Amsterdam, I knew in my heart it would give us more time to get to know each other. And, I was back in the driver's seat. I had given ALL my power to this person I had just found, because of feeling so guilty at giving her away. I needed to get over it. I was no longer ashamed over Liddie's relinquishment. Sad maybe, but I did not feel the shame I once did. I was no longer going to try to please. From then on, I was just going to BE.

My friends and family all agreed with my decision not to make the trip. All, except my new friend Chris from Holland, who informed me he had been planning to meet my flight to welcome me to Amsterdam. Tears flowed from the losses my decision created. Not only would I not meet my lost daughter, but I also would not be celebrating my thirty-fifth wedding anniversary in Holland, nor getting to meet Chris.

I slid back into my black hole, dangling in it as if from a bungy cord that had gotten stuck on some object. Thank heavens I had a therapy session scheduled.

Dr. Mantecon had some insight into Liddie. "Since you said Liddie had written to you about having to help her mother take care of the other children growing up," she explained, "she might be afraid she is getting another person to take care of, especially since you sent your emotionally charged letter professing your love to her."

But, I asked, what was I supposed to do when Liddie's letters felt like they were striking out at me?

"Find a suit of armor to wear," was Dr. Mantecon's advice. "This will allow Liddie's stuff to bounce off you. You are taking everything she is saying personally, but you shouldn't because Liddie is lashing out her own stuff that had nothing to do with you."

That seemed easy for her to say. Then I further explained that it felt like I had my hand over a hot burner, as everything I try to do right ended up with me getting burnt. To that, she replied, "Well then, wear an oven mitt!"

As we were saying goodbye, the doctor offered encouraging words. "Just keep on doing what you have been doing, as it has all been done in the name of love and is therefore correct."

But what was correct? In the last two weeks since receiving Liddie's confrontational letter, my emotions had ranged from intense rage to great sadness. I searched deeply, trying to understand why I was so upset, and realized I felt Liddie's statement that I should seek professional help was condescending and digging at my psyche. Emotional sharing was hard for me. But, Liddie's comment made me think she didn't believe I had the common sense to seek out a therapist.

*   *   *   *   *   *   *   *

After a restless night's sleep, I opened my eyes to the quiet of the morning and realized that, by now, Liddie had probably received my letter canceling the trip. I felt numb. Breaking the silence of the morning, the jeweler phoned to inform me the necklace was ready to be picked up. But, I no longer wanted it. Nor did I want any part of birth motherhood any longer!

Putting on my robe and slippers, I went downstairs for my morning coffee and headed for my computer to write again to my friends.

Subject: How I Really Feel About Reunions
Date: 96-08-01
From: SJH
To: Birth mother list.com

Dear Ladies,

It still amazes me when experts in books say you have to be emotionally ready for anything in a reunion. Like ... how do you do that???? You can't think the worst because, if one is honest, you can only hope for the best. I have the feeling everyone wants their reunion to be PERFECT.

Since we are being honest here, I am feeling numb. Even though my mind spins thoughts of this scenario, my feelings are nil. I have shut down, taking a rest.

Don't care if I ever see her. I am sick of being angry, upset, emotional, and obsessed and want my life back the way it was. I am ALMOST sorry I searched. I thought I was doing a good thing and now all I see is hurt and pain on both sides. For what?

Then a little voice tells me ... because some day, having knowledge of me and what I know about my past will help her to become grounded, like building a house that now has a foundation. I might never see it in my lifetime, but I did give this gift with almost no strings. The only string was to meet her once in person. That was acknowledged in my first letter, and accepted by her. This was the goal all along. I went back and reread her letters again and she said, "Since you found me, I think it is up to you to decide where to meet. I will leave it up to you." Right!

I also think my anger right now is having to do with someone who says they don't need to know where they came from to know where they are going. To me, that means she has put her armor on so tightly that this is what she honestly believes. As an adoptee, I understand, as I have done the same thing, but being a birth mother, that statement also means, "I have done very well without you all these years. You gave me up and I dealt with it. While it would be interesting knowing you, I really don't want to get into those feelings right now. My life is full. You can write to me if you wish and I will answer, but don't call, don't come.'"

I am not angry at Liddie. Heck, I don't know her. I am angry at myself for not seeing this coming. I am very, very angry at the son of a bitch who took advantage of me, who caused this all to happen. I am also very, very angry at my birth father who, from what psychics have said, made my mother put me on the porch. How dare he, the coward.

I am angry at a system that branded us as unfit, demanding we give up our babies. To think they put women away in homes to shield them from the public!

Who thought that up? While I was not in one, (had to do things on my own), that just infuriates me. I am angry at myself for never dealing with any of this until now. Just like I am angry at not allowing myself to be angry. Thus.... I am shutting down.

When I hear good reunion stories right now, I cannot respond, since I do not know what that is like. I only pray for all of you searching, that you do not have to go through what I am going through. I hope that your children will live close enough to you to visit them often. I hope they will want to meet you. I WANT to meet my mom.

I realize I have come a long way emotionally this past year, but I feel like the scar, the wound from my relinquishment and my own adoption opening wider and wider. It is not healing. The scar just seems to be ripping wider apart. I wish I could have warm healing water come and flush all this pain away. As it stands now, I have dried blood forming into a pattern of uncertainty, crying out for a miracle medicine to heal.

Thank you for your kind words and bear with me through this. You are all so wise. I think the bottom line is we all want to be loved and respected for who we are. I just wish it were easier.

Sally

CHAPTER TWELVE

A month had passed since Liddie received the letter informing her I was not coming to see her, and she still had not responded. After working through my own feelings, I began to wonder if perhaps I should look to other avenues besides adoption issues to explain Liddie's actions. Could it be that the emotional atmosphere inevitably caused by her adoptive family's experiences with the Holocaust may be causing Liddie's defensiveness?

Liddie had revealed that her adoptive mother lost most of her aunts, uncles and cousins in the Holocaust, and continued to experience "War Trauma." Many adoption issues were actually similar to those of survivors of the Holocaust. Tears from my own losses seemed always to be triggered by listening to stories of the Holocaust. I wondered if her mother might have projected some of the same types of feelings as other survivors had onto their children.

From knowing other adult children of Holocaust survivors, I found they carried extreme feelings of never measuring up and a deep concern for their parent's well being, often to the detriment of not being able to tap into their own feelings and recognize their own life path. I found my observations backed up in *The Shadow of the Holocaust, The Second Generation* by author Aaron Hass. In Hass's study of adult children of Holocaust survivors, three words were reflected by almost every such person the author interviewed: fear, mistrust and cynicism.

If this was the case for Liddie, how would I be able to win her trust? How will she overcome her fear? This might very well be a bigger hurdle than I thought.

Hoping to find my theory of Liddie's reactions to me to be untrue, I called my searcher, who had been a support group leader for over twenty years to get her opinion. Peg did not understand Liddie's reaction because she said she had been reuniting people right and left and all of them wanted to meet. "Often after a reunion, there can be a cooling off period," she said. "But what you are experiencing isn't normal. Maybe you don't want this type of person in your life?"

Her question was never an option. Liddie was my daughter. I gave her away and I needed to be able to tolerate her abuse to make up for my mistake. If Liddie needed a target for her anger, then I was willing. How could I not have Liddie in my life?

* * * * * * * *

While waiting for Liddie's reply, I tried to stay busy and get back to a life of sorts to keep my mind off everything. But I struggled, and needed to write to the women I knew who would understand.

Subject: I want my old life back!!! Help!!!
Date: 96-09-15
From: SJH
To: Birth mother list.com

Dear Ladies,

The time has come for me to try to finish my own search for my birth parents and I have been avoiding it like the plague. What I need to do is search yearbooks in Catholic All Women's colleges (ones that were women's colleges back then) to see if I can find anyone who looks like my birth father, as described by the psychic. I researched the names of such colleges a year ago, got their addresses and phone numbers, pinned the information on my bulletin board and did nothing. Blamed it on my search for Liddie.

My friend in Maryland (who has been helping me) wants me to check the obituaries in the town where I was found to see if anyone mentioned having a priest as a relative that died, since the psychic said he had relatives in the area. I am to check and see if my being found was printed in the *Baltimore Sun*. If it wasn't, then he feels I just might have a birth certificate, since Maryland wouldn't recognize me as being adopted.

Everything is so vague. For the past three years, I have been so excited about doing my search. I had a goal. Now it seems like I am trying to pick out a tiny strand of dark hair sunken in a deep pool of black, dirty oil. Why haven't I called these schools to see if they even have yearbooks? For that matter, why haven't I even made my airline reservation to go back east? How come I didn't even buy a new outfit for my high school reunion? Me, the clothes horse?

Ross and I talked about this and he wanted to know if I was depressed, disappointed, angry, what? I used the word disappointed about my reunion with Liddie. To cover up my disappointment, I have been shopping. Now nothing I bought is out of line, Christmas gifts, garage sales, etc., just something to fill my time. I have tried to get a schedule of normalcy back after such a long time of searching, but I am having a hard time reaching that goal.

My job is as wife and homemaker, but I haven't touched my house in days. Boring. Rather sort buttons, write on the net, or go shopping. Even though the house needs attended to, I don't care. (Well, I do care, but at the moment, I guess not enough.) I haven't touched my piano in months either. What has happened to my get up and go? I want my enthusiasm back.

It is like I am a bottle full of love, anger, mistrust, sadness, yes mostly sadness, knowing the cork holding them might explode at any moment. If it does, it might ruin any relationship I might have with Liddie, so I hold my cork in as tightly as I can. Look what happened when I loosened it a bit, and shared my loving feelings with my daughter. She suggested I seek professional help. I am already doing that and she knew it. What the heck do I do with these pent up feelings? How do I get MYSELF back?

I have put off, until this morning, what I have really been feeling. In a way, why should I look for my parents? They dumped me on that damn porch (oops, the cork eased a little). Am I afraid I will just find more pain? What the heck am I really afraid of? Why can't I seem to get a direction? Why aren't I excited about going east to see my brother and his wife, the beautiful autumn leaves, and see friends I haven't seen in years? At the moment, I just don't care and know I should, as that would be normal for me.

I am thinking I need to go back to my therapist and then wonder what in the world she could do to help. I don't think I am depressed, because I do get up every day and do things, but I KNOW I am avoiding getting back into the search for my birth parents. I also realize I must do it now as my birth mom would be approximately 74 to 75 years of age and might die before I find her. I can't afford to sit and wait until I am in a better emotional place. I only get two weeks a year to do this. Feedback, please.

Sally

The overwhelming suggestion from my friends was to go back to see my therapist. Many felt I should set aside searching for my birth parents, since I was so emotionally involved with my almost reunion with Liddie.

I was lucky to get an appointment with Dr. Mantecon for later that afternoon.

*   *   *   *   *   *   *   *

Through a flood of tears, I told my therapist about the confusing times I had been having. "I think I am going crazy," I told her. "The other day, I had to tear the house apart to find my reading glasses. I found them in the wastebasket! Then, running an errand to a strip mall, I returned to my car to find I had left my car door wide open with my cell phone and tapes in clear view. Next, going to a meeting, I took the wrong freeway, which meant I had to go thirty miles out of my way. I even sat in a restaurant's lobby waiting for my girlfriend for a half hour, until I realized I was a day early. What is going on with me?"

To my surprise, Dr. Mantecon said that everything I was experiencing was normal. "It is called grief," she said.

Tearing at my Kleenex, I told her I knew the five stages of grief, but I didn't remember confusion as one.

"Oh, confusion is a biggie," she responded. "It comes after the anger stage."

Somehow, I was only feeling a little comfort knowing I wasn't crazy. "Why am I so tired all the time," I asked her.

"Oh, that is an easy one to answer, too," she said. "It is because what you are dealing with takes a lot of energy. You are getting hit with losses from both sides now. Allow yourself to cry and mourn."

When, Dr. Mantecon asked if I wanted to make another appointment, I found myself telling her I didn't want one. Mourning I could do at home. I didn't need an appointment to cry!

* * * * * * * *

For the next few weeks, I worked hard at figuring things out. Enlightenment was exhausting. Going deeper within, I realized that, in my mind, I had placed Liddie in a box right after her birth. Psychically, this box was located in my energy space outside my body, to the right side of my aura, and she remained there, with me but not with me, until I heard her voice for the first time.

It was then that Liddie crept into my very being, kicking and screaming, causing my emotions to finally wake up. Still in the box, I could hear her say, "Hello, hello, can you hear me? I am the baby you gave away. See, now I have a Dutch accent and I am all grown up. You gave me away, so now you will have to deal with me from afar." As she kicked her way out of the box and her long silence, my body curled up in pain.

My colon flared up, the ulcers in my mouth returned. Unable to deal any longer with the pain, I thought if I could just put that box outside me again, out in space where it had been for so long, I could be at peace again. It was only then that I realized that my daughter had always been a conscious part of my being. Even when she was in a box she was with me.

Still dragging myself around, having only enough energy to do the bare necessities, I was naturally drawn to a book by Deepak Chopra, MD. entitled *Boundless Energy*. Perhaps there would be a clue to getting my old self back. In his book, Chopra stated that the three most dangerous creators of stress are, "rejection, disappointment and doubt." Well, I certainly had all three.

He continued, "Fatigue was really just a kind of inertia, a physical sense of disappointment with life." How could I not agree with that statement as disappointed as I was with the way my reunion was going? It certainly was not what I had envisioned. On top of that, no progress was being made on the search for my birth parents.

Dr. Chopra also said:

> Chemicals called neuropeptides are produced by the brain every time a thought or feeling occurs. The type of neuropeptides produced correspond to the quality of

> thought or feeling that has taken place. Receptors to neuropeptides have been found throughout the digestive system, the heart, lungs, kidneys and in the immune system as well as the brain.

Now, that I could at least understand my tiredness, I was able continue on, though still somewhat in a fog.

Writing my friend Richard, I told him in my emotionally raw state, I didn't think I wanted to be involved in searching in any major way when I went back east this time. But I still wanted to do something, so I asked him for suggestions.

Richard wrote back expressing his concern. "I think," he said,. that your best bet at this point is to stop searching and take a well needed break. You have found out what you have known for some time now, that searching is a very consuming and exhausting endeavor. The difference is that you have pushed the envelope beyond what you can physically and emotionally handle."

In the shock of letting go, what happened next was strange and frightening. My mind became like a blank video and every so often a picture would flash on the screen of my mind's eye. It was hard to tell exactly what the pictures were as they were fragmented. It was as if I were seeing images of past lives. This continued twenty-four hours a day, often waking me from my sleep. In one, I saw a stranger being beheaded by the guillotine, an image so strong I awoke in a cold sweat.

There were images of someone trying to steal my baby. In it, I was standing all alone, then snow, like what appears when the tape runs past its content came into my head. On and on the tape ran, demanding attention. "Wake up!" it seemed to be saying. "Make your own video, a decent one for yourself. This is the only way you will be able to stop the constant whirling of the old tapes in your brain. Put your life in some sort of order."

But, the question was, how? Were these images symbolic of my feelings? My friend, Jarrett, had described the pain of losing her son to adoption as like the feeling one has of having a phantom limb after an amputation. Part of me was ripped away, yet a phantom remained always reminding me of my loss. For me, it was my box. I was getting scared.

Concerned about me, my Internet friend, Sue, FedExed me a book called *Birth Mother Trauma* by Heather Carlini. In it was a test to take to see if you suffered from any core issues of relinquishment on the list. My answer to most of the questions was "yes."

Had I suffered from low self-esteem? - Yes. Grieved the loss of my child? - Not certain. Had problems forgiving myself and others involved in the relinquishment? - Not certain. Had I been out of touch with my feelings? -Yes. Did I have difficulty giving and receiving love? - Not certain. Did I have problems with codependency? - Yes. I could answer "no" to having self-hatred and dysfunctional sexual problems.

Over the years I had suffered from most of the compulsive behaviors they listed in order to divert the hidden pain especially: excessive smoking, excessive shopping binges, yelling, excessive napping, excessive involvement in community activities, excessive cleaning, and excessive eating chocolate.

I found I had suffered from nearly all of the defense mechanisms over the years: repression, denial, projection, displacement, avoidance, rationalization and intellectualization. Sublimation I was not certain about, and I didn't feel I was ever passive-aggressive.

At one time or another, I had suffered from all the illnesses listed: asthma, allergies, skin problems, stomach problems, backache, unexplained aches and pains, sinus problems, anxiety, panic attacks, chronic depression and cancer (skin).

I hadn't suffered from agoraphobia (fear of certain objects or situations, making the victims housebound). But, I had suffered from claustrophobia.

After taking a personal inventory, I found I had suffered from all of the emotions listed: anger, shame, remorse, resentment, guilt, hurt, loneliness, numbness and happiness, too.

All of the survival tactics listed I had used over the years: pretending, numbing out, avoidance and denial. Despite all the stress, I had not tried to numb the pain with mind-altering substances like alcohol, anti-depressants, tranquilizers, prescription drugs, illegal drugs or food, thank heavens.

As the author said, you can only work on a problem when you know the full extent of the problem. I certainly had a clear picture now.

In a private post, another birth mother friend suggested that, since I was struggling so hard emotionally, I might consider taking an anti-depressant drug. "Sometimes the brain needs a rest," she said. "Even though you are functioning, you are still depressed." My friend Ric joked, "Take them and get some for me!"

Perhaps it was time for that sort of help. God knows, I had tried all the normal avenues in order to get better: co-dependency groups, birthmother-adoptee support groups, an adoption therapist, and psychics. I had talked it out, written it out and attended conferences. I had read books to try to understand, but still my pain kept escalating.

Yet, I felt weak having to ask for a crutch. But, I knew that asking for help was the first step toward recovery, and decided to reach out. The walk across the room to phone the doctor felt like a long mile. But, tired of not sleeping, of having no energy, of being continually sad, I picked up the phone and called Dr. Mirkil for an appointment.

The medication Zoloft was what he prescribed, and, soon after taking it, I was finally able to get a good night's sleep.

I could tolerate the sweats that were a side effect, because suddenly I had energy. Now, I could look back over the past three years and realize just how far I had come.

* * * * * * * *

Feeling better, I dashed around and got Liddie's thirty-seventh birthday presents off in the mail, packed my bags and was off on my trip to Pennsylvania.

However, when I arrived at my brother and sister-in-law's house, I realized how emotionally fragile I still was. All I wanted to do was be with them.

One evening, needing to get out of the house, but not wanting to venture far from their home, I took a drive to my old neighborhood a few blocks away. As I drove by the house I grew up in, I was reminded of how life changes.

Glancing in the window to the only room lit, I saw the new family sitting round their dining room table creating their own memories, the same way my family did for fifty years. The glow from the room illuminated the darkness of the black night, emphasizing the loss I felt for my adoptive parents.

When I returned to my brother's house, I learned that the lady I had been named after had just passed away, and that my best girlfriend Donna was in the hospital for a radical mastectomy. Life, while always precious, seemed fragile all of a sudden.

Visiting Donna in her hospital room before leaving, I noticed a framed picture by her bedside of Donna and her children standing with her now deceased parents. Even in the dim light of the room, their resemblance to each other was unmistaken. Family was Donna's security in her time of fear and pain. I would never be able to put a picture of my birth parents in a frame, draw strength from our familiarity. Overwhelmed with this deeper realization of my loss and with my concern for Donna, I had to cut short my visit and hurry out of the room. It was all too much to bear.

On the plane back home to California, I had to face the fact that I was not going to ever find my birth parents. The little bit of research I had done at the York Historical Society during my visit had shown me how futile my search was.

* * * * * * * *

"Like most things in life, reunion is not an event: It is a process." Reading Pat Taylor's words in the October CUB Communicator, I had to agree. A lovely letter had arrived from Liddie stating that she had called to wish me a happy birthday. Unfortunately, I missed her call since I was in Pennsylvania, but I felt it was a great breakthrough. It was the first time she had ever called me, and to wish me a happy birthday! Our reunion was back on track.

Was it my new medication or just time passing that made me feel differently about my reunion? For one thing, I was no longer obsessed about receiving a letter from her. Still, my insecurities lingered, not allowing me a moment's peace it seemed. Thoughts like Liddie already has a mother and father, or, you don't fit into her life anywhere, continually pounded their way into my head. Except, while these thoughts made me sad, I was not falling apart over them.

My birth mother friends kept my insecurities in check by reminding me I did fit into her life, and, when we finally met, I would know that for certain. Secretly, though, I said to myself that if we met fine, and if we didn't that would be fine, too. But, was this just a rationalization to keep me from getting hurt?

Each night I went to sleep thinking about Liddie, wondering what she was doing. Each morning upon awakening, I would say a silent hello to her picture now in its new frame. One morning I awoke with memories of the time I was pregnant with her and began comparing that pregnancy with my experiences carrying my three sons.

With my sons, I read everything I could get my hands on concerning pregnancy and the latest techniques in delivery. One brand new technique I opted for. A large bubble-type contraction was placed on my belly during labor. Whenever a contraction would begin, I pushed a button and the bubble created a vacuum that lifted up my skin and muscles, allowing the baby to move freely down the birth canal and eliminating much of the muscle pain.

Completely pampered by my husband during my pregnancies with my sons, I was able to buy beautiful maternity clothes. The nursery was decorated and infant clothes abounded. I even had a baby shower. They were exciting times and so normal.

With Liddie, everything had been planned or scheduled by someone else, and I followed blindly along. No baby books, no baby things. Support money was taken from the birth father by the agency and given to me. Everything was decided or done for me, as if I were carrying a pot of gold.

My best interests were never considered. The focus of any support was on the product I was carrying to insure its healthy delivery to the people paying, whom the agency felt more worthy. All I had to do is sit on the rough, durable old couch in my rented, furnished basement apartment and watch the constant television. All the while, I patted my belly and communed with my daughter. Despite the hardship, it was a time I completely cherished.

How could I have been so naive as to not have investigated my pregnancy? At the time, I thought that all I needed to do was take my vitamins and all would be fine. No one ever prepared me for the actual process of delivery. All I knew to draw from was what I had seen on television, which was usually the onset of labor and then the miraculous delivery. My mother did tell me to "act like a lady and not yell like some women did when in labor." I tried to obey.

That morning it had been one year since receiving Liddie's first letter. Ironically, this was the day that Disney Studios chose to re-release the movie Bambi on video. Dashing to the store to purchase a copy, I wondered if it would still have the same impact on me that it did as a small child. It took a few weeks to work up the courage to actually view it. When I did I found myself laughing at parts I didn't remember.

But at the scene with Bambi calling out for his murdered mother, "Mother where are you? Mother, Mother where are you?" my memories flooded in. As a child I had identified with Bambi in my longing for my birth mother. When I named my daughter Bambi, I was naming another lost soul.

* * * * * * * *

After watching the film, I needed to resume my search for my birth parents. First, I placed a call to Mount Saint Mary's College in Maryland. My girl friend Donna felt this could be the school my parents came from, since it was located directly on the route to the house where I was found. Perhaps they would have a 1938-39 yearbook I could borrow.

My fear that Catholics would be reluctant to give out information about one of their own was unfounded. The caring person answering my questions about the school said there were no yearbooks from that time period, but that a priest teaching at the school during that time would indeed have lived right on campus.

So, I gave her a brief physical description of the birth father, the name Mary Teresa Sennett that the psychic had come up with, as well as the other names various people had conjured for me over the years. The woman at the college, Barbara, was very willing to do some research for me.

Suddenly, my search was being supported again. My friend Reenie sent a special crystal for me to keep with me to help in my search process. The crystal must have had special powers because things started happening.

The following Monday morning after receiving Reenie's gift, *People Magazine* called wanting to do a story on my being a foundling. They talked with me for an hour. Before hanging up, the reporter arranged for a time for the photographer to come take my picture. When I got off the phone, I was shaking, and was surprised that it was still so upsetting to relive my beginnings and my search. Suddenly, I felt vulnerable at the thought of having my story so public.

Then, Richard introduced me to his Uncle Dave who was a psychic, saying his uncle should be able to shed some light on my search. After corresponding with Richard for nearly two years, I was surprised that I was only now getting this lead. Richard said to be persistent when calling, because his uncle didn't have an answering machine. Writing the number on a post-it note, I promptly lost it.

A few weeks later, Barbara from Mount Saint Mary's College phoned saying she could not find a Mary Teresa Sennett among her list of nuns. She only found one priest with a middle name of Patrick and was sending a copy of his photo. In addition, she was going to send a list of all the priests in the Harrisburg and Baltimore diocese for the years 1938-39. I quickly sent out a check to cover the photocopying expenses.

* * * * * * * *

It would be tulip season soon in Holland, and my urge to finally meet Liddie became extremely strong. But our relationship continued to be tenuous, and I hesitated to bring up the possibility of a visit. I didn't want to rock the boat on the progress we had made so far. Why would Liddie want to meet me anyway?

As I considered the possibility, I remembered about Uncle Dave and called Richard for his number. Pinning the post-it with it to the bulletin board this time, I promptly forgot about it. But, then a few weeks later, I awoke with a commanding voice in my head saying, "Today is the day you must call Uncle Dave." With coffee cup in hand, I retrieved the number from the bulletin board, calmly walked over to the phone and dialed his number.

His voice was pleasant and I said a silent prayer of thanksgiving he was there to talk. We visited for two hours. Fortunately, I was using the free Friday phone line. After hanging up, I dashed to the computer to relay the conversation to my friends online.

Subject: Sally's New Search Findings via Psychic
Date: 97-07-03
From: SJH
To: Birth mother list.com

Dear Ladies,

At this moment, I am exhilarated and exhausted. I just got off the phone with the psychic I was to call. He is my (Internet) friend Richard's uncle. I have had his number for a while. This morning when I opened my eyes, my inner voice told me today was the day to call. When I did, I found him just walking into his house and was a little out of breath. I offered to call him back, but he wouldn't hear of it.

I introduced myself and told him how I had received his phone number and why I was calling. We talked for almost two hours, not about my search the whole time, but events and people he has located in the past. I found him to be a wonderful, interesting person. This is exactly what he said to me. Much he confirmed from what the other psychics have said, but he was also able to clarify other information and add some new things, too. O.K. Here goes.

"In 1937, your mother met your father. This year, 1937, is an important year. Your father was of the clergy, but did not remain a priest and in fact, could have married your mother. He was between 25 and 35 years of age when you were born. Your mother was 16 or 17. I keep getting twenty-five miles from the school where you were left or the place they had their rendezvous or were from. It is toward the Atlantic Ocean."

He told me to check the list of names I will be getting from Mount Saint Mary's to see which ones got married and how I was to do that was to check the marriage records. I am not sure about how to do this, but it is a place to restart my search.

Then he told me the name I have been searching for the past two years, Mary Teresa Sennet is wrong, well kind of. The Mary Teresa part is correct, but the last name is Center or Centura or a derivative of the name Center. He feels it would be spelled in Italian, French, or Spanish, since that, is my nationality. No matter how they spelled Center, the first vowel would be an 'e.' Then he said, "Your father was indeed Irish or was from the British Isles."

A midwife delivered you and since she was well known in the area at that time, she should be easy to find. She would have written down the facts of your birth. The car seen dropping you off was a three-year-old Plymouth."

Now get a load of this. My real birthday is January 27, just like the other psychic in Pennsylvania told me last year. I was born just after midnight that day. I got to thinking. My daughter was born the twenty-seventh, too. I was born 1939, Liddie, 1959. Am I seeing a pattern here? I just realized I was born on a Thursday. Liddie was born on a Tuesday.

What he said next made me sad. He said your mom had you with her for two full weekends before putting you on that porch. You had on booties with pink ribbons strung through them and someone has them, kept them. They might be lost by now, but INSIDE THEM was a note from your mother telling you she loved you, that she was being forced to do this and she didn't want to do it." (I had a note from my mother? I want it!) What he said makes sense, as the paper said I was from one to two weeks old when found, so that fits.

He went on to say, "All the women in your family, generation after generation, look alike so you should look for someone who looks like you." I told him Liddie did look very much like me. If this is the case, I will devour year books for someone who looks like me."

When talking about my visit to the house where I was left and how emotional I got, he said, "That is because your mother left part of her cells there and when you returned, you picked them up."

When I asked him why my story wasn't picked to be in *People Magazine*, he said, "Your information, when made public, would have really stung someone badly."

He said I should have my DNA done. Why, I don't know? He also felt ancestral graves needed to be investigated and that he and his nephew Richard could do that. "We could find a name that way," he said. He explained his technique for pinpointing exactly where my birth parents graves would be.

Before hanging up, he stressed to me that I was not an unwanted child; that my purpose in life would be manifested through my children. I hung up, paced awhile, looked at my calendar and realized it was Good Friday. I then walked to my kitchen sink and saw all the blossoms on my Easter lily had popped open while I was on the phone with Uncle Dave, the ones that had been tightly closed all week. I dropped my jaw in awe. Life truly does continue.

Sally

*   *   *   *   *   *   *   *

During trying times, it seemed I always found answers in books. Back in the library for more inspiration, I discovered profound wisdom in Viktor E. Frankl's book, *Man's Search for Meaning*.

> To live is to suffer, to survive is to find meaning in the suffering. No man can tell another what this purpose is. Each must find out for him self and must accept responsibility that his answer prescribes. If he succeeds, he will continue to grow in spite of all indignities.

Frankl also stated that, "An abnormal reaction to an abnormal situation is normal behavior."

Could it be that all birth mothers who were not given choices did, in fact, act normal by hiding their child's relinquishment for all these years?

CHAPTER THIRTEEN

One day, while visiting my choral director's house, I noticed his framed, ornate birth certificate hanging on the wall and got the idea to frame mine, too. Back at home, digging through our safe to find it, I uncovered an envelope marked 'Sally Stuff.' Thinking my certificate must be in it, I dumped the contents out on the floor. Instead of finding the certificate, I found a letter addressed to my mother's sister, my Aunt Rachel.

Opening it, I realized it was a letter my adoptive mother had written to her twin sister after bringing me home from the hospital. For some reason, I could not recall ever seeing the letter. My brother must have sent it after closing up my parent's affairs. It was written on a Monday morning, March 13, 1939.

> Dearest Family,
>
> It's really happened! Judy is now soundly sleeping in her little bed at 125 W. Louther Street and is she sweet? And are my kids excited! Alverta, our nanny just gave her ten o'clock bottle and I asked her to bring her up afterwards so the children might see her. The nursery school children know she's downstairs in the baby bed and we have had an epidemic of chronic 'trots' all morning. I forbid them to go into her room but we're still watching them carefully just the same. I think they go down and peek in the door. All they can see is the bed, but I'm not going to trust them too far.
>
> She certainly looks different in her own little clothes and her eyes are bright and shiny. Ethel and

Russell went with us to York and they think she's very bright. She has beautiful hands and feet. Her little head is shaping out nicely and she has a dimple in her left cheek. Ethel says she has the hands of a fine musician.

She is on a very simple formula: Carnation milk, sterile water and Beta Lactose. They had her on Lactogen but she didn't thrive as she should have, so Dr. Smyser, the pediatrician who was taking care of her in the hospital, changed to this formula. He's written out directions to follow until she is four months old. She is also to have two tablespoons of orange juice twice a day and viosterol, but if our doctor says we can, after he examines her, we're going to change to cod liver oil as they have recently debunked viosterol.

And, Rachel, she is a model of behavior so far. We arrived home safely at five o'clock and she slept the whole way home, even tho it was an hour over her suppertime. We fed her and put her to bed and she fussed a little bit and went to sleep. At eight I fed her again, changed her and had her up to be admired, then put her back to bed and she slept till eleven when I undressed her and greased her well with camphorated oil (she still has a tiny cough, but no cold), fed her and put her to bed for the night. At two-thirty, in her sleep, I fed her and changed her and put her back again 'till ten when Alverta went through this process again and she slept 'till one. I bathed her and played with her till two-thirty then put her back again.

She is a healthy little mite doing all the proper things at the right time. Maybe six weeks in the hospital does that for them. She is a darling and I am so anxious for you to see her. When are you coming down? Seems she's been sent to take Mary Carolyn's place. I love her already, but she's been getting all the rest and I couldn't sleep last night. I was too excited.

Lots of love,

From Us

To see the name of the doctor and realize this was the very same doctor I had such strong feelings about when I looked at the York Hospital's 100th Anniversary book, was shocking and exciting. To think I actually knew at some level. But, I was also sad to have it confirmed that I really was a replacement for Mary Caroline, their first child that had died. My suspicions had not been a figment of my imagination. How could they have ever truly loved me when I wasn't her?

Still on my hands and knees, I continued to dig through the contents of the floor safe and found a large envelope that I remembered now held my baptismal certificate. Anticipating an ornate piece of paper I could frame, I was shocked to see that the document was marred. Where it said "name of child," a thick black line was drawn through the word "child." Replacing the word "child" was the word "ADOPTED." I couldn't hang such a thing! I felt like I had been struck by a canon ball.

Crumpled on the floor, tears flowing, I knew what a concentration camp survivor must feel, their number tattooed on their arm for the whole world to see. Only my damn 'adopted' label was tattooed onto my soul, where no one could see. Each individual's memories hidden, each creating a masquerade of their real selves.

* * * * * * * *

Fired up with thoughts about adoption, I wondered when I was going to hear from the courts concerning my request for my relinquishment papers. No sooner had the thought crossed my mind and the phone rang with my answer. Tonya from the Ingham County Probate Court in Lansing, Michigan was calling. Judge Economy was releasing my surrender papers, but first the court needed a dollar fifty. Annoyed, but knowing I needed a court order to have what was mine released to me, I quickly made out the check and sent it. If for a mere dollar fifty, I can get proof of my dastardly deed, so be it.

Randy Zimmerman, the head of records for the Pennsylvania State Police called, answering my request for further information on my abandonment. He informed me, "I am sorry to tell you this, but the only records kept longer than twenty-five years are unsolved deaths. Those are kept on file for seventy-five years. I am extremely sorry I can't be of help, but I think you have done an admirable search."

Then he added, "I will be at this number until January when I retire, but I have a lot of friends here and they can contact me at home, as I am willing to help you investigate. Anything you need concerning your case, please give me a call."

Hanging up the phone, my heart felt heavy. Genealogists felt I had records somewhere, and I had so hoped the police would have them. Maybe this was a sign for me to stop searching? But there was still a tiny, very tiny glimmer of hope that there might be something on the list Barbara was sending from Mount Saint Mary's. Then I could lead my own investigation. But when, I wondered, was I going to let this search go?

My pessimistic thoughts lasted only a few days, until I received an interesting picture in the mail. Immediately, I wrote my birth mother friends on line.

Subject: My Bmom. Yes or no? Confused!
Date: 97-06-21
From: SJHX
To: Birth mother's list.com

Dear Ladies,

I received the most interesting letter today. I had written to Rev. Senft's church, asking for a picture of Rev. and Mrs. Senft. Not wanting to bother the Senft's at their retirement home, I figured the church secretary could photo copy their picture from their church directory and send it to me. The current minister at the church, probably worried about privacy laws, forwarded my letter on to the Senfts.

In my letter I told them I was writing a book and wanted to add their picture, (but what I really wanted was a picture of Mrs. Senft so I could see what she looked like). Rev. Senft returned my original letter, writing a few lines across the bottom of the page saying they were glad to hear from me again. They also enclosed a lovely picture of the two of them.

When I looked at their signature I about died! His wife's name was Irene. (The first psychic saw the name Irene.)

Another psychic had said, "I see your mother coming from the Baltimore area, but I didn't realize her name was Irene! Knowing Rev. Senft graduated from the Gettysburg Lutheran Seminary, not far from where I was found, does have me wondering.

The problem is, I got no special feeling looking at their picture. I figure they wouldn't have sent their picture to me if they were my birth parents, would they? I wonder how I can find out if she could be my mom? If she is, I doubt the Rev. knows anything about it. Irene is very pretty and aged well. I wouldn't mind having her as my mother.

Sally

At first I didn't connect the great uneasiness I was feeling with having received the picture of the Senfts. My children arrived from Reno and San Francisco to take part in a wedding, and only part of me could feel happy being with them for the four days. The other half of me was in turmoil. By the time everyone left, I had a serious attack of ulcers in my mouth, which really frightened me, since I had not had such an attack since beginning my medication. Was

I beginning to go back into my black hole again? Was this just a pity party for one?

I wasn't even sure it was the picture. It was just that I had received such a "hit" when I read her name, that I wanted the same strong feeling when I saw her picture. I had it propped up against a picture frame on top of my computer table, and hoped, by staring at it long enough, I would feel something, anything. Was Irene meant to be my fantasy mom? Was that why I received the picture?

Meanwhile, my relinquishment papers arrived. Why now? Reluctantly, I opened the envelope, preparing myself to read the words I had never seen before, words that stated I had given up my rights to be Liddie's mother.

Actually, the words were not what upset me, as it turned out, as much as the date the document was signed. November 2, 1959 was only six days after having Liddie! My signature at the bottom had the letters tightly squeezed together, clearly showing my despair. Usually, my signature is free flowing. Nor had I used my legal name, Sara, instead signing it Sally Jeanette Miller.

Flipping the document over, I noticed it was headed 'Content of Guardian Ad Litem.' By signing it, I gave the agency permission to act as my guardian ad litem. The guardian's name apparently was Dorothy Johnson. But, who the hell was she? All this was new to me, as I never knew anyone was acting as my guardian.

They hadn't even spelled my name correctly, typing two 'n's' in Jeannette, instead of one the way I spelled it. Proof they really didn't know me, nor did they really care to. Was all this really legal then? But, what difference did it make now?

The next paper changed my life:

STATE OF MICHIGAN

THE PROBATE COURT FOR THE COUNTY OF WAYNE

STATE OF MICHIGAN

COUNTY OF WAYNE RELEASE OF CHILD

I, Sally Jeannette Miller of the city of Ypsilanti, county of Washtenaw, State of Michigan, being of the age of 20 years and respectively and the mother of an illegitimate child named Bambi Lynn Miller born of the 27th of October A.D., 1959, the city of Detroit ... county of Wayne ... state of Michigan, and being solicitous that said child be cared for or placed in a suitable home by adoption or otherwise under the laws of the State of Michigan, so hereby of my own free will and accord fully release and surrender the child to the Michigan Children's Aid Society, Detroit, Michigan, a licensee under Act #47, 1st extra session of 1944. I hereby certify that the undersigned referee duly authorized by law to administer oaths did first fully explain to me my legal rights in the premises concerning said child and concerning said adoption and did fully appraise me of the fact that I need not execute this release unless I desire so to do of my free will and accord, but that once having executed this release I thereby lose any and all rights in, to and concerning said child, forever.

In witness whereof, I have hereunto set my hand and seal this 2nd day of November A.D., 1959.

Signed, sealed and delivered in presence of:

(in very faint letters) Mrs. Wessinger (the social worker)

(another signature I couldn't read)

Sally Jeannette Miller (Seal)

Laying my reading glasses down, I gazed out the window. Never did I remember them telling me I could legally change my mind about giving up my daughter.

When I signed the papers, they had already taken my baby. So, I didn't think I had the right to change my mind.

All I remember was the invisible yet very real impenetrable wall I put up around myself, the wall finally clanging firmly closed and locked as I lifted the pen from signing the document. Perhaps this was what I had to do in order to survive. But, I had not only erected the wall, I added three more locks to be certain it was secure, puttied any cracks so there could be no seepage, no entrance. Now, all these years later, I was realizing I had locked myself in, too.

*   *   *   *   *   *   *   *

My physical symptoms were telling me it was time to again work on my feelings. But, instead of staying with them, I decided to go to the library to do more research.

Hungry, I stopped by the local diner to grab something to eat. A thin, long-haired, scruffy looking tattooed man sat down a few seats from me and ordered a cup of coffee. At first, I thought he might be homeless or have a mental problem, so I ignored him. But, when he started up a conversation, I discovered inside his gruff-looking body was a very interesting person. He told me he was a native of San Juan Capistrano, but now lived on an Indian reservation near San Diego. He had just given a speech in the area and stopped for lunch. After we talked for a while, he told me he had the power to heal. "I am also psychic," he said. "But, I never take money for my gift."

Another psychic person had entered my life! But, now I knew there was no such thing as a coincidence, so I asked him what he saw concerning the picture of Irene.

His reply was, "If you didn't get any feelings from the picture, then you have the wrong Irene. Let it go. It will resolve itself.

Pausing before taking a bite of my sandwich, I wondered why it was that when someone else tells you what you already know deep down, only then does it make sense?

*   *   *   *   *   *   *   *

To put the last of my nagging doubts aside, that Mrs. Senft was my mother, I wrote her a letter.

> Dear Mrs. Senft,
>
> I am going to take an emotional risk here and come out and ask you if you are my birth mother. I need to write this letter to put my mind at ease, as I must, for my own physical health, finish this aspect of my search. Please let me explain why I feel this is possible.
>
> First, my Aunt Rachel whom you know always said you just had to be my natural mother as we looked so much alike. That was the reason I contacted you in the first place, way back in 1984. Then in 1994, I restarted my search. I have now met or been in contact with all parties involved in my abandonment. All new information has been investigated. Feeling at a dead end, psychics entered my life, giving me information that again brought my thoughts back to you. This is what they said:
>
> 1. Mother comes from Baltimore area.
> 2. I see religious overtones surrounding the car seen dropping you off. Someone involved with the clergy.
> 3. Mother was approx. 5’4” tall
> 4. I see the name Irene as the mother
>
> You seem to fit all the above. As I stare at your beautiful face, I so want for you to be my birth mom, while at the same time, I wouldn’t stick this label on you if it weren’t true. What is so weird to me

is that we do have the same mouth, cheek bones and appear to have the same taste in clothes. If you in fact are not my mom, then if it is all right, you will be my fantasy mom. The one I have been searching for.

For my book, please tell me a little about you and your husband, such as the year you were married and what times were like back then. What are your hobbies? How many children do you have? What are their ages and what do they do? Anything you think would be of interest to my readers. Have you ever run across people with the last name of Center, or a Mary Teresa Center? Remember, you are very important to my story as you got me to the people who found me.

Thank you for letting me be honest. You are very pretty and I would be proud to have you related to me.

Sincerely,

Sally Howard

About a week later, I received a lengthy, lovely, but shocking letter back from Irene. She began by saying, "I'll answer your letter as forthrightly as you asked it. No, I am NOT your mother. I was a virgin until the day I married. In a Christian family in the forties, this was customary."

Making the NOT in big letters and explaining the 'virgin thing,' I found interesting. Apparently, when I was born in 1939, Irene was not yet married. She was very fertile, too, since she had seven children. She could have been my mom.

"Irene," she wrote, "was a very common name in the Baltimore area." But, my jaw dropped when she said she had attended an all girl's high school, just not a Catholic one.

In addition to loving sports, her hobbies were, "smocking little dresses, machine quilting and counted cross stitch, cooking, especially baking." Her letter ended, "I'm sorry for your sake that I don't fulfill your hopes and dreams, but you are entitled to any fantasies you desire. You are welcome to visit us anytime you are back east."

As I laid my letter down, I realized my search was now over. It was time to write my natural mother that good-bye letter, the one I had procrastinated doing for almost sixty years. Pen in hand, I wrote:

Dear Mom,

I am so sorry I wasn't able to stay in the warmth of your arms that cold February evening. I really did want to stay with you. I am glad that you put me in a pretty dress and wrapped me in a few blankets, but I still got cold. I did not like being in that paper bag either, as it was deep and dark in there and I missed you.

When I got to the hospital, the nurses named me Judy because they didn't know what else to call me. You must have breast fed me as I sure didn't like their formula. I have been told I lost a lot of weight those six weeks I was in thc hospital while they searched for you. I guess I wanted your familiar smell and touch. Did you know the police searched for you?

Why did you put that ink mark on my leg? Was it so you would know it was your child that was found? Was it so you could identify me? A psychic man Dave told me you wrote me a note and stuck it in my booties telling me you loved me. Maybe it was then that the ink got on my leg? I never got your note. I am sorry you were forced to give me up. I think you would have liked me.

I don't know what to tell you about my life except that I have been very lucky. Professional people adopted me, thus I grew up enjoying a good middle class life. I had problems with my adoptive mom because I knew she wasn't you. While I know she worked very hard at being a good mom, we were never able to really connect. Something always seemed to get in the way of closeness. She did teach me to enjoy the arts: music, art, dance and I have found a deep enjoyment with them in my life. They somehow touch my soul.

Did you realize I was born in the year of the Tiger? I kind of act like that sometimes, especially when I see the underdog being mistreated. I have always worked in the Social Service field, trying to make a difference while here on earth. I love being around people. Guess I am curious about their lives, since I feel mine is rather made up. Kind of puts everything in perspective.

I have been married for over 40 years and have three wonderful sons and a daughter I gave up for adoption, just like you did to me. Adopt, adapt. I hate those words. I wish I could have been the well-adjusted child but I couldn't because I wanted you, mom. All these years, I have yearned to mend our severed umbilical cord, to become connected again in some way. While I know that is hard for people who aren't adopted to understand, I know you will know what I mean.

Do I have any brothers or sisters? Liddie, my daughter, the one I found, looks a lot like me. More so than my boys. Wouldn't it be neat if we could take one of those four generations of women pictures, as Liddie has two little girls and I have a granddaughter with one of my sons? The picture would show six females all genetically connected together.

Since I know I will never, ever see you in my lifetime, please know that I love you and do not hold anything against you for giving me away. I ache to have your arms around me, and since you can't do that, I will imagine it happening. I hope and pray you had a happy life and most of all, that you found peace.

Love,

Your daughter, Sally

Was I supposed to feel better now? All the psychologists said this letter was necessary. Well, I don't feel great. In fact, I feel empty. It feels like

I failed in my attempt to do something. I am also a little angry my dream of being reunited with my mom has ended. Why couldn't she have searched for me? Why did I have to do all the work? I am also a little frightened to say goodbye to my obsessive behavior, created by my continual searching for the past four years, a behavior of which I am now very familiar.

CHAPTER FOURTEEN

While I sat at my computer playing a game to take my mind off things, my husband poked his head into the room and surprised me by wondering when I wanted to go to Amsterdam. "I need dates," he said.

As soon as we decided October 9 was a good time, panic set in. As I sat at my computer, I typed in 'PARALYZED' on my screen. I was paralyzed with fear. When a few days later Ross dropped the airline tickets on the table in front of me, I knew there was no turning back. We were really going!

There was too much to think about. Soon, I was having my upset stomachs again. I was either sleeping too much or not enough. Anytime anyone asked, "Aren't you getting excited about seeing your daughter?" I shut down. My brain's "elevator" did not want to stop on that floor. What was wrong with me?

Instead of thinking, I began doing, shopping for items to bring the girls: Liddie, Jet and Cato. Soon, I had a huge pile of presents, all needing to be wrapped in either birthday or Christmas paper. Having nothing to transport all of them in, I purchased a duffel bag on wheels that hopefully would be capable of holding everything.

The pile of gifts called out to me to wrap them. But, each day, I walked by the pile but couldn't make myself do it. Looking at the gifts triggered my strains of doubt. Liddie must be dreading our first meeting as much as I was. Would it be like the uncomfortable feeling of walking into a party and finding no one there you know? Was my discomfort from a fear that I wouldn't measure up, that I would perhaps say something to upset her? I couldn't wait for that first meeting to be over with. Then, hopefully, things would be a little more relaxed.

But, what if I'm jet lagged and my mind won't be able to think clearly from a lack of sleep? This, the most important trip of my life! What kind of clothes should I take? Which shoes? Would I need a long coat or a short one? God, I wish I were thinner! Twenty years younger, too. I was torturing myself. Ross said I was having an anxiety attack and should not worry about such trivial things. If only my stomach would stop hurting.

For days I toured the malls and discount stores for a new outfit to wear. Everyone always feels better in something new. But, I found nothing that could make me look twenty years younger or twenty pounds thinner. What was causing me to be so hung up on the clothes I would wear? Finally I realized, if I had my emotional self together, clothes would be the last thing on my mind. With that insight, I decided to bring what I already owned.

Now that my bags were packed, I found something else to worry me. My newly filled and still sensitive tooth might need root canal. As if that were not enough to keep me off center, I began to worry about the plane crashing and never getting to meet Liddie. What if Ross were to get sick and be unable to go with me? I needed his support! What I needed was an anxiety pill, but I didn't want to indulge myself. At least, thank heavens, all the presents fit into the new duffel bag. One worry eliminated.

Finally airborne, I shouldn't have been surprised at my frequent trips to the ladies room, which was always a sign that I was nervous. Like a little child, I kept asking Ross, "What time is it now? What time is it in Amsterdam?" The trip seemed endless. When we finally arrived, there was no one there to meet us, which was a strange feeling.

But then my Internet friend, Chris, arrived. He had been running a little late. Even though I knew she wouldn't, I had still held out hope that Liddie would meet our plane. So, Chris had me walk back among all the people waiting for passengers who were still going through customs, just to be sure. After a cup of coffee, so we could get to know each other better, Chris hauled us, and our luggage, in his tiny car to our hotel.

Once we got settled in our room, I glanced at my watch and realized it was four in the afternoon. Having been up for twenty-four hours, I longed to dive into bed. But, I knew if I did, I would never be able to adjust to the time change. As I lay across the bed and thought about sleeping, Ross barked at me, "You have to call Liddie. She needs to know we have arrived."

With reluctance, I crawled off the bed and began digging into the outside pocket of my suitcase where I knew I had put my address book. But, there was no address book to be found! Even emptying my suitcase produced nothing.

Panic set in as I had no idea what her phone number was or her boyfriend's last name. As I paced the room, I kept saying over and over, "Oh, my God, oh, my God! How could I have left something so important at home?" This was so unlike me as I am always so organized. I felt like I must be losing my mind.

Grabbing the Amsterdam phone book from the nightstand, I found Liddie's phone number was not listed. No wonder she was upset with me for getting her phone number. "OK, Sally," I said to myself. "Be calm. Find her business phone listing. Breathe!" Her business listing was no where to be found.

My world had come to an end. But, then Ross remembered Chris had given me his business card in case there were problems while there. Digging through the contents of my suitcase, now spread all over the bed, I couldn't find Chris's card either!

Thinking it could be in my purse, I turned it upside down and its contents flew out everywhere. Out floated his card. It seemed like a miracle.
My call went through just as he was pulling up in front of their house. Learning of my tale of woe, he rushed to his computer and produced the necessary information.

Swallowing hard, I called Liddie's business. After my call was transferred, I suddenly heard, "Liddie here." Thank heavens I remembered to breathe. After I told her about my crises with her number, she asked if I had received her flowers. Puzzled, I said no.

Liddie explained that she had flowers and a gift delivered to the hotel, and they were to be given to me upon arrival. In her card was a note with her phone number with a request that I call her at work. "I thought I might come by the hotel around 4:45 this afternoon," she said. "We can have a drink and talk." Of course, I told her that would be great.

The room started to swirl, as I realized I would be meeting my daughter in less than thirty minutes.

I asked Ross to go downstairs and check what happened to the flowers and gift, and to also scout out places we might go for a drink. Some place quiet. When the door closed on him, I stood alone, frozen and wondering what to do next?

Panicking, I thought that she couldn't see me for the first time in my traveling outfit. And there was no time for a shower to freshen up. I thought I would throw up! Clothes began flying around the room, until I decided on my three piece black pant suit which was not wrinkled, thank heavens. Switching my gold jewelry to silver, I touched up my make up the best I could. By then I was electrically charged. Just as I gathered myself and took a deep breath, Ross arrived with the beautiful flower arrangement and gift from Liddie.

Yellow roses along with all sorts of flowers I didn't recognize filled the glass vase. Her present was an umbrella. She said in her note that I would be needing it. What a classy thing to do!

With fifteen minutes left to wait after all those years, my anxiety got the best of me, and I thought I was going to literally pass out. Pacing back and forth, I pronounced out loud that I was not going to be sick, simply not going to be sick! "Oh, God," I continued to say over and over. Out loud I prayed, "God, please keep me together. Please don't let me cry and act stupid. Glancing at my watch, I saw that my only daughter was about to arrive. "Breathe, Sally. Breathe!"

The phone rang, jarring my panic attack. Liddie was downstairs. I asked her if she wanted to come up to the room, and she said, "Yes."

Suddenly, my motherly instincts took over as I tried to imagine what it must be like for her to be coming up to my room. If I were she, I would feel like I was walking a tightrope. A nurturing calm came over me. I wanted to help her feel less strange. I stood by my open hotel room door to welcome her. And then there she was, looking so small and very familiar. I felt off balance at seeing someone who looked so much like me.

When she reached the entrance to the room, I asked if I could give her a hug. Taking her slight nod as a sign a hug was OK, I embraced her. The hug was unsuccessful, as Liddie was so stiff. More movement could have been had from hugging a stuffed animal.

We each picked a spot to sit in the room. Liddie chose a chair in the corner by the window. I draped myself across one of the beds nearest her chair, while Ross leaned against the dresser.

We chatted a while, with me talking way too much about nothing. My son, Dan, had warned me to watch out for my tendency to chatter mindlessly when I'm nervous. Later, I learned from Liddie that, when she is nervous, she clams up. So, not being able to stand the silence, I talked even more. The tension in the room was electric. I was grateful that Ross was there to jump in when the conversation got quiet.

At my suggestion, we went downstairs for a drink. Afraid to drink alcohol in case I would say something stupid, I ordered coffee. Liddie had juice, since she was pregnant again. With our conversation lagging, and noticing it was starting to rain, we suggested she should be on her way, since she had ridden her bike.

But, before she left, we made arrangements for our next visit. Liddie decided it would be nice if we came to their house the following afternoon around two o'clock, which would allow her time to do her weekly grocery shopping and allow us to sleep in. After saying goodbye, Ross and I went across the street for a lovely pasta dinner with wine, after which I was finally able to collapse into that 'yearned for' bed.

As I closed my eyes, I thought about the last few hours of finally meeting my daughter. It was the most surreal experience to talk to someone who made me feel like I was talking to myself in the mirror. We hadn't taken pictures, as it would have broken the spell. My emotions frozen, my brain unable to compute, I fell into a deep sleep.

* * * * * * * *

Saturday at Liddie's house was a big day, one that would stay with me forever. We arrived promptly at two o'clock by cab at Liddie's place. Dragging our duffel bag on wheels packed full of presents for everyone, Ross and I both looked at each other with dismay as we faced the narrow winding stairs we would need to tread to reach Liddie's third floor flat. When he heard our suitcase thumping up the wooden stairs, Arjan , her boyfriend, came out to help us.

As I walked into Liddie's flat, I saw my granddaughter Jet (pronounced 'yet') for the very first time. She was sitting in the corner of the living room coloring and not about to have anything to do with us. But, within a few minutes, she thawed, so I dug into the duffel bag and gave her birthday presents to her.

As we talked over wine and snacks, I gave Liddie the scrap/memory book I made for her. She seemed to like it, as she and Arjan quickly looked through it, promising to go through it in detail later.

Soon the baby Cato (pronounced ca-toe) got up from her nap and we were introduced. Liddie then asked if I would like to see some of her pictures.

The first album she showed me took me by surprise. Instead of it being of her growing up, it was of her pregnancy with Jet. What a gift to see my daughter pregnant and about to deliver. While it was a weird feeling, at the same time it was very intimate.

Ross walked over to see what we were looking at and said, "Oops!" Realizing this was girl stuff, he returned to the living room. But, I took in my shock. Never seeing Liddie naked as a baby, I was suddenly seeing her naked all grown up, and pregnant. Just before delivering each child, always at home, she has a picture taken completely naked. I guessed that it was to enable each child to see themselves inside their mother.

Then Liddie did something very special. She shared the ultra sound picture of the baby she was carrying. I was one of the first to see it. In so many ultrasound images, it is so hard to see the baby. But, in this one, I could clearly see it. Wow! Liddie was eleven weeks pregnant. The baby was lying on its back, legs up, a head, a spine and everything.

When I asked if she had any pictures of herself growing up, Liddie pulled another album from the closet. Inviting us for dinner, she said she planned to serve something that took a long time to cook, so I suggested we both go into the kitchen. That way, I could browse through the book and keep her company at the same time. Most of the pictures were taken during her teenage years. She told me she had been in a movie once. I found everything about our conversation so amazingly interesting.

With Ross and Arjan gone for a walk, Liddie and I had time alone to really talk. While making her dessert, she told me she and her mother had big problems during her teenage years, so much so that she left home at the age of seventeen to live with her boyfriend. Liddie said, "I was glad to leave, and my mother was glad to be rid of me. So, it was a mutual thing. In 1990, after my mother's sister (one of the ones her mother moved to Amsterdam to take care of) killed herself, my mother told my adopted sister and I that she didn't want to be a mother to girls anymore, as it was too much of a responsibility and too much of an emotional expenditure."

I could hardly imagine such a thing!

Afterwards, Liddie said she did keep in contact with her father, who would only call when her mother was not at home. Not liking that, Liddie insisted he call when her mother was present. But, when her father told her mother Liddie was pregnant with her first child, her mother suddenly wanted back into her life. Turning from the sink and looking at me with conviction in her eyes, Liddie said, "If there was to be a relationship, it would be on my terms only." Apparently, they saw each other, but not often. In all the photo albums I had looked at, I had seen only one picture of her mom and was surprised at her attractive appearance.

After a lovely meal, it was time to give the kids a bath. Jet asked me to keep her company while she played in the tub, thrilling me to death. Then, Liddie asked me to dry and dress Jet while she took care of Cato. When I forgot to put the undershirt on under her nightgown, Jet said, "undercutter," or something like that in Dutch. Realizing I still had a piece of clothing in my hand, I took off the nightgown and added the undershirt. Ah, perfect.

Having a just bathed child in night clothes snuggled up next to me, ready for a bedtime story, always made me feel all warm and fuzzy. And, to think this was my new found granddaughter!

Sitting cuddled on the couch together, Jet and I read the book I had given her. While I read in English, Jet pretended to read in Dutch. Each of the girls gave me a big good night kiss before going to bed. After watching a video of the family at their new summer house, it was time to call it a day. Returning to the hotel, I felt very close to my daughter. Who needed sleep? I was in love.

* * * * * * * *

Sunday, Ross and I took the boat tour of the canal, and in the evening I called to thank Liddie for the lovely day at her house. During our conversation, she asked what we planned to do Monday. When I told her we thought we would visit the Jewish section of Amsterdam, she suggested we meet for lunch, since her office was in the same area. We could meet at the Rembrandt house.

As I waited for Liddie's arrival, I was in awe realizing that Rembrandt had once lived in the exact house where we were standing. Ross spotted Liddie first from a distance. I asked him how he could tell from so far away, and he said, "That's easy. She walks just like you."

While waiting in a nearby cafe for lunch, we put our hands up against each others and discovered they were the exact same size. Then, in walked Liddie's best girl friend, Edna, camera in hand, to join us for lunch.

As I listened to the two young women talk and giggle, I learned that Liddie hated math in school as much as I did.

She also hated gym the same as me. Here I was back in the 'just like me' thing again. After an hour and a half lunch, they went back to work and we continued to tour.

* * * * * * * *

It was on Tuesday, while walking along the canals sightseeing, that peace enveloped me. The feeling grew from my stomach and radiated throughout my body, causing a calm, warm feeling, despite the cold of the day. As I kept walking, I knew this must be the feeling one gets when successfully completing a search journey, but it was a feeling I wasn't expecting. To me, it signified that I had come full circle, and it felt so right.

* * * * * * * *

The next evening, I called Liddie to make plans for our prearranged dinner engagement. She told me she had made reservations at her favorite restaurant for Wednesday evening, the night before we were scheduled to leave. I just couldn't wait to be with her again. It proved to be a very emotional evening.

Ross and I decided to take it easy during the day Wednesday and visit only one museum, the Rijksmuseum. Exhausted from doing so much walking, we even treated ourselves to a cab. For some reason, I was feeling very unsettled all day. I suspected something was going to come up at dinner, perhaps about her father. Up until then, each time I asked, she said she had no questions.

While getting ready for dinner, I reached into the outside pocket of my suitcase for something and there was my address book, reappearing on the eve of our departure! After dressing, I paced, had a hot flash and paced some more. Another anxiety attack. Even Ross seemed anxious too, as he was ready to go fifteen minutes ahead of time. I made him sit with me in the lobby of the hotel for a while before catching a cab, as I didn't want to get to the restaurant too early.

Taking a deep breath, I finally realized it was time to go. The cab dropped us off outside an elegant and small restaurant. The menu was all in Dutch or French, which led me to believe that they did not cater to tourists. Liddie read each entree to us in English, making faces while describing calf brains, tongue and other meats. We all settled for a gourmet vegetarian meal, which she had preordered for themselves. It was a wonderful choice.

Throughout the three-and-a-half hour dinner, we discussed many things, such as their work, why Liddie chose literature, and especially Russian literature, as her major in college. Her explanation was that it was the least boring, "boring" a word she used often.

I found her Arjan was an absolute darling, but piercing with his questions. But, then, interviewing was what he did for a living. While we waited for dessert, he asked me what this trip meant to me. When I responded that I had had a wonderful time, that wasn't what he wanted to hear. So he asked me again, "I mean, what did this trip mean to YOU?"

As I looked at him sitting across from me, I responded, "This trip has caused me to have a peace I didn't know I was capable of having. I see that Liddie is happy, is loved by a wonderful man, has two adorable children and pregnant with her third. She has a job she loves, and seems to have lots of long time girlfriends. All this gives me great joy, because I know she is happy. What else is there in life, but to be loved and to have a great interest in life, to create fulfillment? My heart is at peace."

From my point of view, I went on to tell him, I had come to believe the theory that children choose their parents, not the other way around. "Maybe Liddie needed to go to the parents she did, so she could be the person she is now," I said. "I went to a mother who abused me, but this in turn gave me great compassion for others, something I might not have had if I had been adopted by someone else. As far as I am concerned, everyone in life is equal. No matter if someone has more powers than I have or more money, for example, each individual has something to offer me. No one is better than anyone else."

Dessert arrived. I had ordered the crème Brule. Just as I inserted my spoon into the crusty top, the question I had been dreading was finally voiced out loud. Liddie asked, "The only question I have left is the one you said you preferred to tell me in person."

Looking at Ross, my heart beating like it might for someone about to go on stage on opening night at the theater, I grabbed my glass of wine and took a sip, giving myself a few more seconds to think and to remind myself not to use the word rape, but instead say I was forced.

Tears poured down my cheeks and onto my lap, as I told her the story of her conception the best way I could without hurting her more. Embarrassed to be crying at the table, I couldn't look at anyone, while I told the story. Lifting my head, finally looking at my daughter, I said, "It was you and me babe. There was no one else. And, then they came and took you away."

Lifting the damp napkin from my lap to soak up more tears, I said, "I never knew how much you weighed or how long you were until I started to search for you and found that information in my hospital records. The only thing I feel I can do now is fight to open records for people who want to find each other. Adoption is sometimes necessary, especially if children are being abused. But, their records must go with them."

Wanting to thank Liddie's mother for passing along my letter, I asked Liddie if she minded if I wrote to her mom. "I don't want you to feel uncomfortable, like having to hide me," I said. "I'm tired of secrets."

But, Liddie didn't want me to write her mom. She said not to worry about it as she didn't really care what her mom thought.

At this point, I figured I might as well go for broke, and told Liddie about the necklace; of how the cantor named her in Hebrew, legitimizing her birth for the first time in the eyes of God. "Your Hebrew name is Lebah Miriam Sarah, and the initials can be your Hebrew name or yours and my first initial," I told her. Taking the necklace from my purse, I handed it to her.

After looking at it a while, she said, "I want you to wear it, as it will remind you of us."

Reassuring her that I would love to wear it, but that it was hers, I told her I would keep it for when she might want it. Ross thought Liddie had a lot of class the way she handled it.

By now, it was almost eleven o'clock, and Liddie had a baby sitter that needed to get home. After calling a cab, we stood outside by the canal. With the engine of the cab warming the air that surrounded us, we said our goodbyes. As Arjan leaned down to give me a hug, I whispered to him, "Take care of my girl." He promised he would. Liddie kissed me on both cheeks and said, "Next year in Jerusalem."

Looking through the rear window of the cab as we drove away, I watched my grown daughter's figure get smaller and smaller and cried my eyes out. I felt so badly having to tell her she was a product of rape. She didn't deserve that. My tears continued throughout the night. I told Ross my birth mother friends had told me I would cry, but I didn't believe them. Now here I was bawling my eyes out. Ross just said he knew I would cry.

*　　*　　*　　*　　*　　*　　*　　*

Boarding the plane the next morning, I realized there was nothing more I could do. Liddie knew everything. Hopefully, she knew I didn't find her to intrude, but because I needed to know she was all right and happy.

When I got home, I was terribly jet lagged but happy to be safe and sound. The first day back, I couldn't even think straight, so I did manual labor like washing the clothes, watering plants, going through the stack of mail. The next day, knowing my birth mother friends from the Internet were dying to find out, I began a three part installment of my story, one installment a day. Their support, I told them, was invaluable.

Ross told me over and over that my trip was very successful, as he was able to observe everything. I made him tell me this daily.

Since arriving home, I had been mostly teary eyed, especially when hearing the name 'mother' in any context on television. Some were the tears that were held in check much of the time in Amsterdam. Now they were thawing, little by little.

* * * * * * * *

Soon I was feeling on a more even keel and, very satisfied that I searched for and got to meet Liddie. It felt like I had my life back, one that now included my long lost daughter. Despite feeling whole finally, the injustice of all that I had to go through, the relinquishment and the search, still lingered.

One evening, in a pensive mood, I gathered my thoughts and my just filled glass of wine and headed for my gazebo. Getting comfortable in my wicker chair, I noticed a jasmine vine wrapping its way around one of the gazebo posts, and wondered if I should pull it off. No, I decided I liked the way it looked there. A butterfly, busy fluttering among the flowers, appeared to be living life to its fullest.

Staring at a large intricate spider web woven between two trees, I could not help relating its fine strands to adoption. When you walk through a web like that, everything changes. Each thread seemed to represent the different stages of searching I had gone through: grief, denial, anger, bargaining, depression, acceptance and of course confusion and its tributaries. A rippling effect. My feelings concerning adoption reminded me of the fly caught in the middle of the web, necessary for the spider, but not thrilling for the fly.

Light from the last of the sunset caught Liddie's necklace. I would wear it for her until she was ready.

AFTERWORD

To celebrate finishing my manuscript, I took a walk around the Dana Point Harbor, delighted to see that no one was sitting on my favorite bench overlooking the ocean. Gazing at the waves, crashing against the rocks of the jetty, I sat enjoying the solitude, mesmerized by the endlessly moving water. Suddenly, something caught the corner of my eye. Looking back at the jetty, I saw a woman standing alone at its highest peak. I hadn't noticed her before. How had she come to be there?

The wind whipping her gauze-like white dress reminded me of the wooden female statues found on the bow of ancient ships. She seemed to be looking directly at me, trying to communicate something. I stared at her, transfixed, hoping to understand the message she seemed to be trying to convey. Something profound was happening, but all I could concentrate on was her safety. I was worried she might slip off the rocks into the ocean. Hadn't she seen the warning signs stating, "no trespassing?" Turning away and blinking my eyes, now burning from staring so long, I again looked back toward the jetty. The figure had vanished, just disappeared. It all seemed so otherworldly.

Shaken, I rushed home and called the psychic who had given me a productive reading a few years ago, during the search for my mother. Not telling her about the vision at the jetty, instead I told her I just finished writing a book and wanted to ask her one last time if she had any more information about my birth mother. She responded, "I see your mother all dressed in white. She is either a nurse or she has passed over to the other side. I get that a Paul Ferrelli took your mother from the area. They relocated in an Italian neighborhood, to a place in New

Jersey where you have visited - a place you have a strong attachment to. He had a son Frank. Your mother had no children of her own."

The only place I had a strong attachment to in New Jersey was Ocean City, where my family vacationed while I was growing up. A quick inquiry into the name Ferrelli led nowhere. Another dead end.

Born from a paper bag. How was I ever to find me?

The information the psychic had given me had made me sad, and I called a friend just to talk things out. Her response was to call a friend of hers from Oregon who had the gift of being able to see the "other side." "It is time you know the truth," she said. "Paula will see something that could put everything to rest for you."

Without hesitating, I placed the call. After Paula and I talked briefly, she suddenly said, "Your mother has passed over. I am so sorry. I hate giving people such information when they are searching. I wish I could give you a name, but these never come to me." We talked a bit more, and then she said, "I can't believe this! I'm getting a name. I never get names! I see the name of Marguerite Gagliardi. She died October 24, 1998 in New Haven Connecticut."

Amazingly, I was able to verify that a woman with that name had died on that date in New Haven. But, she would have been much too old to have been my mother. Something prodded me to go a bit further, and I found a Mary T. Gagliardi, who had died in the same area only a month later, on November 23, 1998. Her age would have matched. Could this be the Mary Teresa I had been searching for all these years? Somehow, it didn't seem to matter anymore. My mother was dead.

But, then I realized that I had found her. She had appeared to me from the rocks of the jetty. That woman standing on the rocks was my mother, and she had come to say goodbye. When she had put me on that porch in a brown paper bag, she had lovingly wrapped me in warm clothes. She never wanted to give me away. She just had no choice. I forgave her finally.

And, I now forgave my adoptive mother. As I came to understand her past, I saw she had done her best in raising me and loved me in her own way the best shc knew how. My adoptive family had given me good values to live my life by, and a brother and sister to love.

Through finding and meeting my daughter and seeing, in her, the mirror image of myself, missing for fifty years, I was finally able to feel connected to my unknown past. I could be at peace with that.

We all need to feel connected to our birth in some way. We need to know our family of origin to solve the mystery of ourselves. But, perhaps the loss of my mother brought me the gift of understanding our eternal connections with each other. She really did come to say goodbye to me from that jetty.

BIBLIOGRAPHY

Henry J Aigner Jr., *Adoption in America Coming of Age.* Larkspur, CA.: Paradigm Press, 1992.

Florence La Rose Ames, Ph.D. *That Sovereign Knowledge -York Hospital's 100 Anniversary.* From Original notes.

John Bowlby, *Attachment and Loss. Volume 1.* N.Y.: Basic Books, Inc., 1969.

John Bowlby, *Attachment & Loss, Volume 11, Separation: Anxiety and Anger.* N.Y. Basic Books.

John Bowlby, *Attachment and Loss. Volume 111, Loss, Sadness and Depression.* N.Y. Basic Books, Inc, 1980.

T. Berry Brazelton, M.D. and Bertrand Cramer, M.D., *The Earliest Relationship.* Reading, Massachusetts: Addison-Wesley Publishing Company, 1990.

Heather Carlini, *Birthmother Trauma-A Counseling Guide for Birth Mothers.* Canada: Scott Printing, 1992.

Deepak Chopra, M. D. *Boundless Energy.* N.Y.: Harmony Books, 1995.

Viktor E. Frankl, *Man's Seach For Meaning-An Introduction to Logotherapy.* Viktor E. Frankl. 4th edition. Boston, Massachusetts: Beacon Press, 1992.

Aaron Hass, *In the Shadow of the Holocaust-The Second Generation.* Ithaca, N.Y.: Cornell University Press, 1990.

Marshall H. Klaus, M.D., Phyllis H. Klaus, M Ed., S.C.W. *The Amazing Newborn.* Reading, Massachusetts.: Addison-Wesley Publishing Company, 1985.

Marshall H. Klaus, M.D., John H. Kennell, M.D., Phyllis H. Klaus, S.C.W., M.F.C.C., *Bonding-Building the Foundations of Secure Attachment and Independence.* Reading, Massachusetts: Addison-Wesley Publishing Company, 1995.

Douglas T. Miller and Marion Nowak, *The Fifties-The Way*

We Really Were. Garden City, N.Y.: Doubleday and Company, 1975-77.

Leonard Nemoy, *You and I*. Millbrae, Ca.: Celestial Arts, 1973.

Peter B. Neubauer, M. D., Alexander Neubauer, *Nature's Thumbprint*. Reading, Massachusetts: Addison-Wesley Publishing Company, Inc. 1990.

Linda T. Sanford, *Strong at Broken Places*. N.Y.: Random House, Inc. 1990.

LaVonne Harper Stiffler, *Synchronicity and Reunion-The Genetic Connection of Adoptees and Birthparents*. Florida: FEA Publishing, 1992.

Patricia E. Taylor, *The Shadow Train*. Baltimore, Maryland: Gateway Press, Inc., 1995.

Nancy Newton Verrier, *Primal Wound*. Baltimore, Maryland: Gateway Press, Inc., 1993.

Robin Warshaw, *I Never Called It Rape.-The MS Report on Recognizing, Fighting and Surviving Date and Acquaintance Rape*. New York, N.Y.: Harper and Row Publishers, Inc. 1988.

Nancy Ziegenmeyer, *Taking Back My Life*. N.Y.: Summit Books, 1992.

NEWSPAPERS, NEWLETTERS, MISC.

The Gazette and Daily, York, Pa. Feb. 7, 1939.

York Dispatch, Feb. 5, 1940.

1794 Walking Tour-200 Years-1794 to 1994. Washington In Carlisle. Phamplet.

Historical Directory of Carlisle, Pa. Carlisle Chamber of Commerce. Phamplet.

Evening Sentinel, Carlisle, Pa. Vol. LV11. No 47, January 29, 1939 and Vol. LIX No 40. January 29, 1940.

Carlisle History print out, Cumberland County Historical Society.

CERA Conference Brochures. "Shedding Light on the Adoption Experience." 1995.

Orange Coast Magazine by Eileen Lenson, July 1995.

Cub Communicator Newsletter, "What's Going on In Adoption Today." Highlights taken from talks given by Reubin Pannor at 1993, 1994 Cub Conferences, June, 1995.

Cub Communicator –Pat Taylor-October, 1996.

New York Times, Dec. 12, 1994-reprinted in *Access* newsletter, Winter, 1995.

OTHER BOOKS THAT HELPED DURING MY SEARCH:

FOR THE BIRTH MOTHER:

Lorraine Dusky, *Birthmark.*
Judith S. Gediman, *Birthbond: Reunions between Birthparents and Adoptees- What happens after.*
Merry Block Jones, *Birth Mothers: Women Who Have Relinquished Babies For Adoption Tell Their Stories.*
Adrienne Rich, *Of Woman Born-Motherhood as Experience and Institution.*
Patricia Roles, *Saying Goodbye to a Baby.*
Carol Schaefer, *The Other Mother..*
Jean A .S. Strauss, *Birthright: The Guide to Search and Reunion for Adoptees Birthparents, and Adoptive Parents.*
Judith Viorst, *Necessary Losses.*
Jan L. Waldron, *Giving Away Simone..*

FOR THE ADOPTEE and ADOPTIVE PARENT:

Robert Anderson, M.D. *Second Choice: Growing up Adopted.*
Jayne Askin, *Search: A Handbook for Adoptees and Birthparents.*
Eric Blau, *Stories of Adoption: Loss and Reunion.*
John Bradshaw, *Family Secrets-What You Don't Know Can Hurt You.*
David M. Brodzinsky, *Being Adopted: The Lifelong Search for Self.*
Heather Carlini, *Adoptee Trauma-A Counseling Guide for Adoptees.*

Betty Jean Lifton, *Journey of the Adopted Self: A Quest for Wholeness.*

Betty Jean Lifton, *Lost and Found: The Adoption Experience.*

Jeanne Lindsay and Catherine Monserrat, *Adoption Awareness-A Guide for Teachers, Counselors, Nurses and Caring Others.*

Michelle McColm, *Adoption Reunions: A Book For Adoptees, Birth Parents and Adoptive Families.*

Marlou Russell, *Adoption Wisdom: A Guide to the Issues and Feelings of Adoption.*

Jayne Schooler, *Searching for a Past: The Adopted Adult's Unique Process of Finding Identity.*

Joe Soll, *Adoption Healing-A path to recovery.*

Arthur D. Sorosky, *The Adoption Triangle: Sealed or Opened Records: How They Affect Adoptees, Birth Parents, and Adoptive Parents.*

Dorothy W. Smith and Laurie Nehls Sherwen, *Mothers and their Adopted Children-The Bonding Process.*

Katarina Wegar, Adoption, Identity and Kinship.

MISC. BOOKS AND NEWSLETTERS:

Linda Braswell, *Quest for Respect-A Healing Guide for Survivors of Rape.*

Jone Carlson, The U.S.A. Search Resources Directory.

Lynn-Claire Davis, *People searching News*

David Gelernter, *1939-The Lost World of the Fair.*

Ted L. Gunderson, *How to Locate Anyone Anywhere.*

Kelli Peduzzi, America in the 20th Century: 1940-49.

Joan Rivers, *Bouncing Back-I've Survived Everything, and I Mean Everything and You Can Too.*

Carolyn Kott Washburne, *America In the 20th Century-1930-39.*

Brian L. Weiss, M.D. *Through Time Into Healing.*

Jon Kabat-Zinn, *Wherever You Go There You Are.*

About the Author

Sally Howard

With a degree in Human Services, Sally started her involvement in the mental health field in Lansing, Michigan. Her recent involvement in the mental health community has been as a Patient Rights Advocate, representing patients being held against their will in mental hospitals in South Orange County, California.

A member of the support group Full Circle, she has been an advocate for open records. A moderator for an adoption internet chat session, a member of an internet birthmother list, a member of AAC and CUB and a speaker on adoption, she has also been a community leader and former president of many organizations.

As a wife, mother and grandmother, she now sells children's books on the Internet. In her spare time, she enjoys, besides writing, singing in her community choir, volunteering at her local library, enjoying the Red Hat Society events and making collage cards.